The Marsh Hen

By Brooke Meanley

Natural History of the King Rail
Natural History of the Swainson's Warbler
Swamps, River Bottoms, and Canebreaks
The Great Dismal Swamp
Birds and Marshes of the Chesapeake Bay Country
Blackwater
Birdlife at Chincoteague
Waterfowl of the Chesapeake Bay Country
The Marsh Hen

The Marsh Hen

A Natural History of the Clapper Rail of the Atlantic Coast Salt Marsh

By Brooke Meanley

With drawings by
John W. Taylor

Tidewater Publishers
Centreville, Maryland

Library of Congress Cataloging in Publication Data

Meanley, Brooke.
    The marsh hen.

    Bibliography: p.
    Includes index.
    1. Clapper rail.   2. Birds—Atlantic Coast (U.S.)
I. Title.
QL696.G876M4   1985   598'.31   84-40825
ISBN 0-87033-332-1

Manufactured in the United States of America
First edition

CONTENTS

ACKNOWLEDGMENTS

I am grateful to the following colleagues of mine in the U.S. Fish and Wildlife Service who have helped in some way in this study: F. M. Uhler, Nancy Coon, Warren Blandin, Matthew C. Perry, G. Michael Haramis, Dan Stotts, John Tauton, and Don Fankhauser. And I wish to thank the following for permission to use material from department reports: Fred Ferrigno of the New Jersey Division of Fish, Game and Wildlife; Hugh A. Bateman, Jr. of the Louisiana Department of Wildlife Fisheries; W. Brock Conrad, Jr. of the South Carolina Wildlife and Marine Resources Department; and Joe Kurz, Game and Fish Division, Georgia Department of Natural Resources. And thanks to Luther C. Goldman, Anthony Florio, Samuel A. Grimes, E. O. Mellinger, and Mark Snyder for the use of several photographs; John W. Taylor for several sketches and the cover illustration; and especially to my wife Anna G. Meanley, for help in editing the manuscript, and assistance in the field work at Chincoteague, Virginia. The photographs are my own unless otherwise indicated.

The Marsh Hen

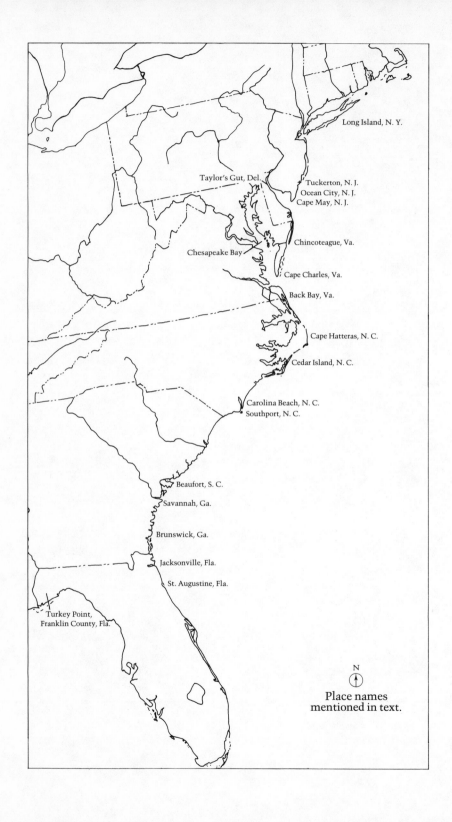

Long Island, N. Y.

Taylor's Gut, Del.

Tuckerton, N. J.
Ocean City, N. J.
Cape May, N. J.

Chincoteague, Va.

Chesapeake Bay

Cape Charles, Va.

Back Bay, Va.

Cape Hatteras, N. C.

Cedar Island, N. C.

Carolina Beach, N. C.
Southport, N. C.

Beaufort, S. C.

Savannah, Ga.

Brunswick, Ga.

Jacksonville, Fla.

St. Augustine, Fla.

Turkey Point,
Franklin County, Fla.

N

Place names
mentioned in text.

INTRODUCTION

The marsh hen or clapper rail is identified more closely than any other bird with the coastal salt marsh. It is a favorite of hunters, watermen, and others who live along the Embayed and the Sea Island sections of the Atlantic Coast, and who are reminded of its presence by its loud discordant calls.

In its salt marsh abode (Fig. 1) the marsh hen or clapper rail is widely distributed, and locally abundant in some sections. Marshall Howe's reference (1982) to the density of willet populations along the Virginia coast can be applied to the marsh hen. Coastal densities are high "because of limited habitat, predictable food supply, and stable water conditions typical of coastal systems."

This study is mostly about the northern clapper rail *(Rallus longirostris crepitans)* of the Northeast and Middle Atlantic coasts, and Wayne's clapper rail *(Rallus longirostris waynei)* of the South Atlantic area. Although it is known to the "coasters" as the marsh hen, I have used the common name clapper rail in most of the text because of comparisons with the closely related king rail *(Rallus elegans)* which, like the clapper, is also locally known as the marsh hen.

Because it is a game bird, most other studies of the clapper rail have been game management oriented. My special interest has been more in the area of rail behavior, with studies made mostly at Chincoteague, Accomack County, Virginia, but also at Taylor's Gut, Kent County, Delaware, and Cameron Parish, Louisiana. Observations of captive clapper rails were made from time of hatching to maturity at the Patuxent Wildlife Research Center, Laurel, Maryland.

Fig. 1. A clapper rail or marsh hen in optimum habitat, the salt marsh. Vegetation is saltmarsh cordgrass (*Spartina alterniflora*). Photograph: Luther C. Goldman.

Some field observations, particularly those of prenesting behavior, were made from an automobile which served as an ideal blind. Such a blind was used to observe the courtship of rails in roadside ditches at Chincoteague and Taylor's Gut. Under these conditions it was possible to distinguish the sexes by their behavior rather than by their appearance, which is similar. The male averages only slightly larger than the female, a difference usually not discernible in the field.

Incorporated into this book are excerpts from studies of other field workers, especially of those conducted in New Jersey, Virginia, North Carolina, South Carolina, Georgia, and Louisiana. Some few sections of this book are based on my own published material that appeared in technical ornithological journals, and a monograph entitled *Natural History of the King Rail* (Meanley, 1969).

The salt marsh habitat of the clapper rail or marsh hen, once thought to be a worthless piece of real estate, is now known to be one of our most valuable natural land-use areas, providing food and shelter for birds, mammals, fishes, and other marine organisms. A strong conservation movement has come along just in time to thwart its rapid destruction.

1.

DISCOVERY AND HISTORY

The saltwater marsh hen, as Audubon called the clapper rail (1835), was discovered in 1783 at Cayenne, French Guiana, on the northeastern coast of South America. In North America, the first clapper rail was described in 1789 from specimens found in a private collection at Hempstead, Long Island, New York.

Alexander Wilson, the pioneer Philadelphia ornithologist, whose career began earlier than Audubon's but overlapped it, knew the clapper rail, as he spent a lot of time in the New Jersey marshes in the late 1700s and early 1800s. In his great work *The American Ornithology*, (1808–14), Wilson did not differentiate between clapper and king rails, apparently thinking the latter to be the adult form of the clapper rail. Wilson's illustration of the clapper rail favors the king rail's brownish plumage.

Elaborating on this point, Audubon, in his account of the king rail (1835, p. 27) and in referring to that species as the Fresh-water Marsh-Hen, stated:

> No doubt exists in my mind that Wilson considered this bird merely the adult *Rallus crepitans*, the manners of which he described, as studied at Great Egg Harbour, New Jersey, while he gave in his works the figure and colouring of the present species. My friend, Thomas Nuttall, has done the same, without I apprehend, having seen the two together. Always unwilling to find fault in so ardent a student of nature as Wilson, I felt almost mortified when, after having in the company of my worthy and learned friend, the Reverend John Bachman, carefully examined the habits of both species, which in form and general appearance, are closely allied, I discovered the error which he had in this instance committed. Independently of the great difference as to size between the two species [actually, there is very little

difference in size], there are circumstances connected with their habits which marks them as distinct. The *Rallus elegans* is altogether a fresh-water bird, while *R. crepitans* never removes from the salt-water marshes.

2.

THE MARSH HEN OR CLAPPER RAIL
BRIEFLY NOTED

The marsh hen or clapper rail, with few exceptions, spends its entire life in the salt marsh, particularly the cordgrass marshes, wandering to the edge from time to time to forage on the mud flats as the tide recedes. Except for the tiny black rail, a bird of varied habitats, other typical rails of the family Rallidae—the king, Virginia, sora, and the yellow—occur mainly in fresh or brackish marshes.

In some localities rails are locally abundant. Although not strictly gregarious, as ornithologist Frank Chapman (1940) points out, they are generally associated through a community of interests. Along the Virginia coast, 79 clapper rail nests were found in a 47-acre tract; and in the early fall thousands of soras flock to fresh tidal river wild rice marshes of the Middle Atlantic coast.

The rails are characterized by their secretive habits; and the yellow and the black rails are probably the two most secretive of the approximately 800 species of North American birds. Because rails are thin or narrow-bodied (whence we get the expression "thin as a rail") they can move deftly through the dense marsh grass without betraying their presence.

Rails are among the most "grounded" families of birds. They seldom fly, unless flushed or harrassed, except during migration. They have developed large strong legs, perhaps at the expense of their short rounded wings. They are surprisingly good swimmers, despite the fact that their feet are not webbed. At peak tides clappers often have to do a lot of swimming to reach areas where they can continue to forage, frequently swimming back and forth across tidal creeks or guts (the latter term is of local use).

Since rails spend much of their time walking or running, they are often described as being weak fliers. And in fact, in some remote parts of the world, species of rails that have lived on predator-free islands for hundreds of years have become flightless. However, the North American rails are strong fliers, as evidenced by their extended migrations from such areas as New Jersey to Florida and from Canada to the Gulf Coast. When flushed in their marsh habitat, they usually fly only a short distance, descending quickly to hide in the cover. I have flushed clapper rails that took off and flew 200 yards or more, and once they gained momentum, were flying as fast as the average wild duck.

In most salt marshes clapper rails live close to a tidal gut where the vegetation is tallest and where most of the fiddler crabs are to be found. Clappers reveal themselves not only by their calls, but by the telltale signs of their tracks, splattered whitish droppings about the size of a 50-cent piece, and often a regurgitated pellet. Willets live in these same marshes, and may leave similar signs, but usually in the more open sections of the marsh.

Rails wander out from the marsh edge to forage in the mud flats and to bathe in the shallows, particularly at low tide. Following a bath they spend a lot of time preening. (I have timed clapper rails as they stood in one spot and preened for 20 to 30 minutes.) They often bathe and preen at dusk, and with the onset of nightfall, move about less, but continue calling. Clapper rails that I have had in captivity settled down for the night, usually sitting with their bodies against the ground. Roth et al. (1972), in their Lousiana radio telemetry study in which transmitters were attached to the backs of clapper rails, found that the birds moved very little at night, even on bright moonlit nights.

Some writers on the subject and most people along the coast state that clapper rail calling is governed to a considerable extent by the changing of the tides, and is often heard at dawn and dusk. They are usually referring to the most commonly known call of the rail, the primary advertising call. I have made a tally of clapper rail calling during all hours of the day and night, and the condition of the tide at the time. On the basis of these entries, I have not been able to associate the primary advertising call or any other of the dozen or so rail calls with a particular stage of the tide. They do seem to call more just after dawn and shortly before dusk. But during the spring courtship period (mainly April and May in Virginia), they often call just as much at night as at any other hour of the day.

As noted in *South Carolina Bird Life* by Sprunt and Chamberlain (1949), "Probably the outstanding characteristic of this bird is its voice; and the wide variety of clacks, grunts, groans, and shrieks which it emits is remarkable. There is one high, grating call which may be given by a bird for fifteen or twenty minutes at a time, repeated with monotonous regularity." The scientific name *Rallus longirostris crepitans* is an apt one, meaning "long-billed clattering rail."

In the clapper rail, sexes are similar in appearance (Fig. 2). Males average slightly larger, a difference not perceived unless birds are weighed and measured, or sexed internally. The average weight of an adult clapper rail is about three-fourths of a pound. From banding studies in New Jersey, it was found that clapper rails may live for at least six years (Banding files, USFWS).

At least 25 subspecies or geographic races have been described throughout its extensive range, which is stretched out along the coast lines from New England to Brazil, including parts of the West Indies, and from San Francisco to Peru. Eight subspecies of clapper rails are recognized in the United States (American Ornithologists' Union, 1957). The northern clapper rail *(Rallus longirostris crepitans)* and Wayne's clapper rail *(R. l. waynei)* of the East Coast, and the mangrove clapper rail *(R. l. insularum)* of the Florida Keys, have a generally grayish plumage. The Louisiana clapper rail *(R. l. saturatus)* of the Gulf Coast, and the California clapper rail *(R. l. obsoletus)* and light-footed clapper rail *(R. l. levipes)* of the California coast are brownish and resemble the king rail. The Yuma clapper rail *(R. l. yumanensis)* of the lower Colorado River valley is also brownish. One form, Scott's clapper rail *(R. l. scottii)*, found along the lower East Coast and the west coast of Florida, is darker than the other clapper subspecies, but its generally brownish plumage resembles that of the king rail.*

---

* See the appendices for further descriptions of subspecies, details of weights and measurements, censusing and trapping methods, and for scientific names of animals and plants mentioned in the text.

Fig. 2. In the clapper rail, sexes are similar in appearance and in size though, on average, males tend to be slightly larger. Photograph: Anthony Florio.

Relationship of Clapper and King Rails

Some ornithologists consider clapper and king rails the same species. The plumages of several clapper subspecies closely resemble that of the king rail, and there is little difference in size, the king averaging slightly larger. But several clapper subspecies also differ slightly in size; and, according to Ridgway and Friedmann (1941), in some there are light and dark phases. Also, the breeding ranges of clapper and king rails overlap in some coastal brackish marshes, and in one marsh there is absolute evidence of interbreeding resulting in the production of viable eggs (Meanley and Wetherbee, 1962).

Dillon Ripley in his monograph, *Rails of the World* (1977), refers to the king rail as a subspecies of the clapper, calling it the king clapper rail; and Ernst Mayr and Lester Short in their study, *Species Taxa of North American Birds* (1970), state that "*Rallus longirostris* and *R. elegans* are respectively saltwater and freshwater forms that replace each other ecologically in eastern North America."

The occurrence of clapper and king rails in the same breeding grounds has been observed by several ornithologists. Robert E. Stewart (personal communication) observed a clapper rail and a king rail together with brood at Chincoteague, Virginia, in June 1951. He has also on numerous occasions observed clapper and king rails togther in the tidal marsh along Ape Hole Creek, a tributary of Pocomoke Sound, Somerset County, Maryland.

In April 1956, I collected a clapper rail and a king rail from the same pond at Grand Chenier, Cameron Parish, Louisiana. In this area, the narrow chenier (a stranded rim of the sea or an old shoreline) serves somewhat as a barrier between the fresh and salt marsh, and these two species merely have to walk a hundred yards or so to be together. It is difficult to separate the two species in the field in the Gulf Coast marshes of Louisiana. The breast of the resident clapper subspecies, *Rallus longirostris saturatus*, is duller brown in contrast to the more rufescent breast color of the king rail. George Lowery (1955) in *Louisiana Birds* also considers the two species as simply ecological representatives of each other.

In the South Atlantic Coast area, Ivan R. Tomkins (1958) encountered a similar situation near Savannah, Georgia. He wrote in his book *The Birdlife of the Savannah River Delta:* "This brackish area, a place of transition from fresh to salt, has some peculiar situations in respect to bird habitats. In the middle of Elba Island I have seen both King and Clapper Rails on territory so close together that both birds were in view at the same time."

At Hog Island, Surry County, Virginia, in the James River opposite historic Jamestown, C. C. Steirly (1959) found both king and clapper rails breeding. Steirly made the following comments about the rail habitat on the island in 1959: "Apparently there is a salinity gradient between the east side of the refuge and the west side of Cobham Bay. Hog Point might be the dividing line. There seems to be a slight difference in the tidal vegetation between the two sides of the refuge although the cord grass marsh seems to be the dominant feature along the east or down river side. The King Rail is most often seen on the west side." In the early 1980s, I found king rails in the cordgrass marsh on the east side where clappers sometimes occur.

On May 18, 1960, John S. Webb and I observed a clapper rail and a king rail together in a brackish tidal marsh along the Smyrna River at Taylor's Gut, Kent County, Delaware. This mated pair was observed on their nesting territory on numerous occasions thereafter and were collected on June 11 (Fig. 3). The nest was also located on that date, and the 5 eggs were removed and placed in an incubator. Despite the fact that optimal incubation conditions were maintained, the embryos died between the seventeenth and nineteenth days of incubation. The embryos appeared to be normal, and deaths were believed to have been accidental rather than indicative of genetic incompatibility.

Subsequent observations revealed that clapper and king rails frequently were found together in the extensive brackish bay marshes in the Taylor's Gut area of Broadway Meadows, located between Fleming's Landing and Woodland Beach, Delaware. Specimens collected from this area showed a wide variation, from typical clapper plumage to typical king plumage.

From my observations, the behavior of the two species is essentially the same with few exceptions. The primary advertising call, that most often associated with both species, and heard throughout the year, is more variable in the clapper rail, and usually given more rapidly. It may be described as a fairly rapid *chac-chac-chac-* or *cac-cac-cac-*, but when occasionally given more slowly, sounds like that delivered by the king rail, *jupe-jupe-jupe-*. In both species, the first notes in the series are louder than succeeding ones, and the tempo increases toward the end of the call when the notes run together. It should be pointed out that my reference to clapper rail calls is based mainly on studies in the Middle Atlantic coast region, where the subspecies or geographic race *crepitans* occurs.

The most striking behavioral difference between the two species is the degreee of tenacity at the nesting site. Incubating clapper rails (Fig. 4) along the Middle Atlantic coast would almost invariably leave the nest well ahead of me as I approached. Occasionally one remained on the nest until I was in sight of it, or would leave and feign injury nearby. However, at most nests, I never saw the bird, and it remained out of sight.

In the first week of June 1984, I located 39 active clapper rail nests at Chincoteague, Virginia, and none of the birds remained

Fig. 3. Mated clapper rail male (right) and king rail female, collected at Taylor's Gut, Kent County, Delaware, June 11, 1960. Their eggs were fertile.

nearby to protest or feign injury. Only one bird made a vocal sound when it left its nest and ran off through the marsh; and of the 35 nests I approached during 1983, only one bird remained in sight, feigning injury 50 feet from the nest. In New Jersey, Kozicky and

Fig. 4. The wind blows the grasses of the nest canopy about from time to time and the incubating bird has to repair the nest.

Schmidt (1949) said that, "As a rule, the bird would leave before the observer approached the nest. A few birds, however, remained on the nest until the observer was within two or three feet, and some feigned injury."

By contrast, the king rail (Fig. 5) in the Arkansas and Louisiana rice fields remained close to the nest most of the time, and sometimes remained on the nest as I approached. On several occasions I was able to catch the incubating bird by hand on the nest and band it, and a number of times I caught the incubating bird on the nest with a long-handled net. On one occasion as I approached a nest at hatching time, the bird flew from the nest and struck me in the chest. At other times birds have struck at my legs or have run to my feet where they remained with wings outstretched. Frequently they feigned injury by spreading their wings, fluttering through the vegetation uttering a distress call, and were virtually always in sight as I examined the nest. My experiences are based on over 100 observations at clapper rail nests and a similar number at king rail nests.

Fig. 5. King rail on nest, Stuttgart, Arkansas.

While the popular literature and most scientific works list the clapper and king rails as distinct species, to some museum taxonomists and others engaged in systematics, the question of whether they are two species or one has remained unanswered.

3.

HABITAT

The Salt Marsh

The coastal salt marshes, abode of the clapper rail, are the last frontier of the eastern United States. They remain the largest parcels of land that have changed the least, and exist today much as they have ever since their substrate emerged from the sea and became a series of salt marshes decked with cordgrass (Fig. 6).

Man has been chipping away at the salt marshes for the past hundred years, filling in and gouging out, but extensive undisturbed areas still exist. In fact, about 2 million acres stretch from the Maine coast to Key West, and several hundred thousand acres border the Gulf Coast (Shaw and Fredine, 1956).

The main body of coastal salt marshes lies between the barrier islands that front on the ocean and the mainland. They either border the embayments behind the barrier islands or fill up most of the in-between area with their solid stands of saltmarsh cordgrass and mosaics of channels and guts through which the tidal waters pass. Extensive stands also border such estuaries as Chesapeake Bay, Delaware Bay, and some of the other embayments near the coast.

This vibrant natural community has been aptly described by Ivan Tomkins in his book, *The Birdlife of the Savannah River Delta* (1958):

> The salt marsh is more than an expanse of cordgrass and black rush. It is a wide expanse of soft wet earths laid over by a skin of grass roots. It is creek edges that are under water at high tides, but strips of mud flats when the tide drops. It has pools entrapped, filled with tidal water or rain water. It is perforated with the holes of fiddler crabs, burrowing

Fig. 6. Salt marsh at low tide in summer. The pure stand of saltmarsh cordgrass (*Spartina alterniflora*) is typical of most of the marshlands along the Atlantic coastal strand. Shrubs at right are high-tide bush *(Iva frutescens)*.

shrimp, and marine worms. The grasses have periwinkle snails attached to their stalks, and when there is dew the whole marsh is a-shimmer with the webs of countless spiders. When the tide comes among the grasses the grasshoppers casually swim from place to place. The marsh changes from hour to hour and from day to day. This day there will be a neap tide that scarcely touches the grass stems, another day the whole marsh is under water for a time; and when it recedes, the turbulent flow carries sediments from the marsh table down into the creeks.

When the marsh plants die, the decomposed material, known as detritus, is assimilated by fiddler crabs and snails, which, in turn, are foods of the clapper rail, whimbrel (Fig. 7), willet (Fig. 8), glossy ibis, and boat-tailed grackle. Decaying marsh grasses, algae, submerged aquatic vegetation, and decomposed bodies of minute marine animals are also utilized by young fin- and shellfish, seeking protection and food in the so-called nursery grounds, the tidal creeks or guts that thread the saltmarsh.

Fig. 7. The whimbrel migrates along the coast, stopping off enroute to forage in the salt marsh and mud flats for crustaceans, mollusks, grasshoppers, and other food items. This large shorebird nests in the arctic tundra and winters in South America. Illustration: John W. Taylor

The predominant vegetation of the coastal salt marsh, salt-marsh cordgrass *(Spartina alterniflora)* grows in uniform stands, but at different heights in different zones. Along some sections of the coast it varies in height from 6 inches to 6 feet. This is due to cordgrass sensitivity to water levels or to elevations of the marsh substrate. The taller cordgrass grows along the edge of tidal guts or creeks, an area that is being constantly flushed and fertilized by the tides. The shortgrass *alterniflora* zone is farther from the gut and in some sections of the marsh intergrades with the salt meadow.

Fig. 8. The willet is a common nesting bird in much of the same Atlantic Coast salt marsh as the clapper rail. However, it usually nests in the salt meadow *(Spartina patens)* behind the taller cordgrass *(S. alterniflora)* zone bordering the tidal guts where the clappers are generally found. Photograph: Luther C. Goldman.

Fig. 9. Saltmeadow cordgrass *(Spartina patens)* in foreground, Elliott Island, Dorchester County, Maryland. Nesting habitat of the black rail. Clapper rails seldom nest in this short and dense marsh grass.

In the higher and drier parts of most salt marshes, the salt meadow is usually the predominant marsh community (Fig. 9). Saltmeadow cordgrass *(Spartina patens)* and saltgrass *(Distichlis spicata)* are the principal species of plants in most of the salt meadows of the Middle Atlantic coast region. Both of these grasses grow to only a foot or so in height, and are usually windblown, thus giving this kind of marsh a meadowlike appearance. The salt meadow is usually covered with water only by spring or flood tides, while much of the saltmarsh cordgrass zone is flooded twice daily. Along the Virginia coast, flood tides during the summer sometimes bring thousands of blue crabs and diamondback terrapins into the marsh.

Extensive stands of needlerush or blackrush *(Juncus roemerianus)*, uniform in height, border sections of saltmarsh cordgrass and salt meadows, usually on the back or landward side of marshes (Fig. 10). This is a rather sterile area for wildlife compared to the other salt marsh plant communities.

Dead marsh grasses and submerged vegetation are carried into the edge of the marsh by an abnormally high tide and, as the tide recedes, are deposited or lodged in the growth of standing salt-

Fig. 10. Uniform stand of needlerush or blackrush *(Juncus roemerianus),* Somerset County, Maryland. Most needlerush marshes have low density populations of nesting clapper rails. Nest and eggs in photograph are marsh hawk's.

marsh cordgrass beside or near a tidal gut. This formation, known as wrack, is a long line of packed debris that extends in a line following the contour of the edge of the marsh, sometimes having the shape of a low serpentine wall. This wall is not always continuous, often occurring in segments, and is usually along the margins of the larger tidal guts. In some areas, nests of laughing gulls and Forster's terns are located on top of the wrack, which is often a foot or so in height and above normal high tide. A clapper rail's nest close by in the tall-growth cordgrass close to the tidal gut is often only 2 or 3 feet from a gull or tern nest located on the wrack.

At Chincoteague, laughing gulls and Forster's terns also nest in pure stands of saltmarsh cordgrass (Figs. 11, 12), but do not attempt to conceal their nests as do the clapper rails, black ducks, and gadwalls (Fig. 13). Willets and seaside and sharp-tailed sparrows usually nest in the salt meadows.

Although the seaside sparrow (Fig. 14) usually nests in the salt meadow, in some respects it is the clapper rail's closest associate, as it spends much of its time foraging in the saltmarsh cordgrass

Fig. 11. Laughing gull on nest in saltmarsh cordgrass zone bordering tidal gut at Chincoteague, Virginia, June 7, 1983. Laughing gulls are colonial nesters frequenting the same habitat as clapper rails. Active gull and rail nests are sometimes less than 6 feet apart. Photograph: Luther C. Goldman.

Fig. 12. Nest and eggs of Forster's tern on wrack in salt marsh next to tidal gut, and 8 feet from clapper rail nest. Chincoteague, Virginia, in late May.

Fig. 13. Nest and eggs of gadwall in saltmarsh cordgrass, Chincoteague, Virginia, in June. Nest was 20 feet from clapper rail nest.

zone bordering the tidal guts, where the clapper occurs most of the time. An example of the close association of the two species will be noted in a breeding bird census conducted by Will Post (1981) near Cedar Keys on the Gulf Coast of Florida. In a 37-acre tract Post found only three species: seaside sparrow (39), clapper rail (9), and marsh wren (1).

The salt marsh is a feeding ground for herons, egrets (Fig. 15), glossy ibises, and migrant shorebirds (Fig. 16) that forage in tidal pools where minnows, small crustaceans, and aquatic insects have been trapped as the tide recedes.

In winter at Chincoteague, the greater snow goose (Fig. 17), boat-tailed grackle (Fig. 18), and clapper rail are the principal species of birds in the rail habitat. The common mammal at all seasons is the field mouse or meadow vole, known locally in some areas as "monk." This mouse often builds its nest under cast-off shells of the horseshoe crab.

The extensive pure salt marshes, particularly those close to the ocean, have fewer mammals and reptiles than brackish and fresh marshes. Amphibians are virtually absent from salt marshes because their tender skin will not endure the salt. Raccoons occasionally wander in from higher ground, and the diamondback

Fig. 14. The seaside sparrow is as closely associated with the salt marsh as the clapper rail. Both species spend virtually their entire lives in this habitat. Photograph: Luther C. Goldman.

terrapin (Fig. 19) is the only reptile that I've seen in the pure stands of saltmarsh cordgrass at Chincoteague.

The salt marsh at Chincoteague takes on a brownish appearance in winter but, while there has been some deterioration, the vegetation stands at nearly the same height as in summer, thus affording adequate cover along the edge of the tidal guts where clapper rails spend most of their time. The brownish aspect con-

Fig. 15. The snowy egret feeds in salt marsh pools and mud flats.

tinues well into April, but shows new growth of about 6 inches by the first week of that month.

The Brackish Marsh

A brackish marsh is simply a less salty marsh, and lies between the fresh and salt marshes. A notable example of a brackish marsh with clapper and king rails is the one at Taylor's Gut in the Smyrna River marshes, Kent County, Delaware (Fig. 20). This wide sweep of marshes is also known as Broadway Meadows. At Taylor's Gut in the early 1960s, the marsh appeared to be more typical of clapper than king habitat (Table 1, p. 31). The dominant plants were saltmarsh cordgrass and saltmarsh bulrush. Hightide-bush bordered the tidal guts. Two miles upstream from Taylor's Gut, at Fleming's Landing, king rails only were observed. The vegetation there was mainly saltmeadow cordgrass and Olney three-square, with small amounts of big cordgrass *(Spartina cynosuroides)*, saltmarsh cordgrass, and hightide-bush.

Two miles toward Delaware Bay from Taylor's Gut, along the Woodland Beach causeway, clapper rails were abundant, but king rails were not observed. Saltmarsh cordgrass was predominant,

Fig. 16. Portrait of a dowitcher, common migrant shorebird along the coast, where it forages in the salt marsh mud flats.

Fig. 17. Most of the greater snow goose population spends the winter in the salt marshes of the Middle Atlantic coast. Greater snows, boat-tailed grackles, and clapper rails are the principal species occurring in the winter salt marsh at Chincoteague, Virginia. Photograph: Matthew C. Perry.

Fig. 18. The boat-tailed grackle is a year-round resident of the Chinco-teague salt marsh and the South Atlantic coastal area (where it is locally known as the "jackdaw"). The Cajuns along the Louisiana Gulf Coast call it the "chock." Illustration courtesy of the U.S. Fish and Wildlife Service.

with lesser amounts of saltmarsh bulrush. Hightide-bush was absent. This area had more typical elements of a salt marsh, with the exception of the presence of small amounts of big cordgrass, a plant associated more with brackish marshes. Salinity readings at Taylor's Gut were intermediate between those at the other two stations (Table 2, p. 31).

Fig. 19. The diamondback terrapin is the only reptile that lives in the salt marsh and bordering tidal guts at Chincoteague, Virginia.

Fig. 20. Brackish marsh habitat of mixed clapper and king rail breeding populations at Taylor's Gut, a tributary of the Smyrna River, near Delaware Bay, Kent County, Delaware. Vegetation mostly *Spartina alterniflora* and *Scirpus robustus*.

Table 1. Plant Composition at Three Stations in Broadway Meadows, Delaware, 1960. *

	Fleming's Landing (king rails only)	Taylor's Gut (both rails)	Woodland Beach (clapper rails only)
Saltmeadow cordgrass	50	trace	0
Saltmarsh cordgrass	15	50	70
Saltmarsh bulrush	0	30	20
Big cordgrass	5	10	10
Olney three-square	25	0	0
Hightide-bush	5	10	0
Saltgrass	trace	trace	0
Groundsel-bush	trace	0	0

Table 2. Salinity Determinations at Three Stations in Broadway Meadows, Delaware, 1960†

	Fleming's Landing	Taylor's Gut	Woodland Beach Causeway
Low Tide	4,380	7,190	7,600
High Tide	3,700	5,670	7,480

Clapper and king rails both were common breeding birds at Taylor's Gut. Other breeding birds there included the red-winged blackbird, swamp sparrow, marsh wren, black duck, seaside sparrow, song sparrow, and least bittern, a good representation of the birds of a brackish marsh in the Middle Atlantic states.

*Percentages based on estimates for five 10-foot quadrants at each station.
†Parts per million. Water samples were analyzed in the Chemistry Laboratory, Patuxent Wildlife Research Center, Laurel, Maryland; sea water salinity is 32,000 to 35,000 ppm.

4.

FOODS AND FEEDING BEHAVIOR

The clapper rail lives in a world of plenty. An abundance of food is virtually always at hand during the summer half of the year, and throughout the year in the Southeast where most of the Atlantic Coast rails winter. There are few habitats in nature that produce the abundance of food found in the coastal salt marsh and bordering tidal guts. Only during an occasional flood tide are clapper rails momentarily deprived; then they often move farther out in the marsh from the tidal guts or into the higher marsh edge to continue their foraging.

Low tide is when the opportunities for feeding are optimal. The fiddler crab colonies (Fig. 21) are completely exposed and marine worms and small clams are easier to obtain. At high tide periwinkle and saltmarsh snails (Fig. 22) climb up the stalks of spartina, as do the grasshoppers and crickets, and all can be picked off easily by the rails.

In most areas of their Atlantic coastal range clapper rails feed to a great extent on crustaceans, particularly the common and square-backed fiddler crabs (Fig. 23). Next on the list are snails, grasshoppers and allied insects, spiders, clams, clam worms, fish, and occasionally seeds of salt marsh plants. Some unusual animal foods found in clapper rail stomachs were mice, a baby diamond-backed terrapin, and the cocoon of a butterfly. At Slidell, Louisiana, a clapper rail stomach contained mainly acorns, probably from a live oak, and along the southwestern Louisiana coast, two birds had eaten domestic rice, indicating they had left their salt or brackish marsh environment to visit the freshwater habitat of a rice field. In the Tijuana salt marsh in California, Jorgensen and

Ferguson (1982) saw a clapper rail catch a live adult Savannah sparrow.

Foods at Wallops Island, Accomack County, Virginia

Wallops Island is an ocean barrier island lying about 5 miles south of Chincoteague. In the early 1900s (mostly 1902, 1911, and 1913), during the period August–November, the stomachs or gizzards of several hundred clapper rails taken by hunters were obtained by the U.S. Biological Survey (now the U.S. Fish and Wildlife Service). Most of these stomachs were examined by Biologist John C. Jones. From this series I randomly selected the reports of the contents of 100 stomachs.

The percentage of food by volume eaten by the rails was as follows: crustaceans (mainly fiddler crabs) formed approximately 50 percent of the food items taken; grasshoppers and allies, about 35 percent; spiders, 5 percent; and miscellaneous insects (including beetles, flies, ichneumids, plant hoppers, and stickbugs), periwinkle snails, and parts of marsh plants made up the remainder of the foods. Seventy-five of the 100 birds ate crustaceans, and 50 ate grasshoppers. Forty-three species of animals and/or plants were represented in the series.

Foods at Gargathy Bay, Accomack County, Virginia

Gargathy Bay lies behind Metomkin Island, an ocean barrier beach, and is located about 15 miles south of Chincoteague. In a series of 80 stomachs from clapper rails taken there in September 1983, the percentages by volume of foods taken were as follows: grasshoppers, 60 percent; fiddler crabs, 20 percent; snails, 10 percent; and crickets and other insects, 10 percent. Fiddlers were present in 55 stomachs; snails in 35; grasshoppers were in 30 stomachs; undetermined insects were present in 10 stomachs; and crickets were in 5. One stomach contained the remains of a mouse (*Microtus* sp.).

Foods in Georgia Coastal Marshes

John Oney (1954) examined the stomachs of 284 clapper rails obtained from hunters in October and November 1947. Fiddler crabs formed approximately 75 perent of the food by volume, of which square-backed fiddler crabs comprised about 54 percent. Periwinkle snails formed 14 percent. One species of square-backed

Fig. 21. Fiddler crabs on mud flat at edge of salt marsh. Fiddlers are an important food of clapper rails, willets, boat-tailed grackles, whimbrels, and several other species of birds of the coastal strand. Photograph: E. O. Mellinger.

Fig. 22. Periwinkle snails climbing up stems of saltmarsh cordgrass as the tide slowly rises in the marsh. They are ingested whole by the clapper rail, and John Oney reports that 48 have been found in a single stomach.

Fig. 23. Regurgitated pellets (top two rows) and foods (except clam) of clapper rail along the Virginia coast. Large pellets are from adult birds; smaller are from 2–4-day-old chicks, and were found in nests. Square-backed fiddler crab *(Sesarma reticulatum)* in lower left-hand corner; salt-marsh snail *(Melampus bidentatus)*, center; common fiddler *(Uca pugnax)* in lower right-hand corner. Clam is from Delaware brackish marsh. Pellets mainly composed of fiddler crab particles. Photograph: Mark Snyder.

fiddler crab *(Sesarma cinereum)* occurred in 58 percent of the 284 stomachs; another *(Sesarma reticulatum)* occurred in 37 percent; and the common fiddler *(Uca* sp.) in 45 percent. Oney found 48 periwinkle snails in one clapper rail stomach.

In a series of 10 stomachs collected by W. W. Worthington from the South Carolina coast, periwinkle snails formed 70 percent of the food by volume, and fiddlers 30 percent.

In both Virginia samples it should be noted that no mention is made of marine worms in the diet of the clapper rail, yet they are taken regularly by this bird. The explanation is that worms are digested so rapidly that remains rarely show up in stomachs; and I have seldom found them in the esophagus. In John Oney's 284-stomach (or gizzard) sample, clam worms occurred only as a trace percentage. But over the years I have spent many hours observing the foraging behavior of clapper rails, and on numerous occasions, usually during low tide, I have seen clapper rails in the tidal flats feeding on marine worms.

Some foods such as grasshoppers are a seasonal item, and at Chincoteague they are numerous in the marshes in late summer and early autumn. I rarely saw a grasshopper in the salt marshes until late July. Live periwinkle snails appear to be available mainly during the summer half of the year in the Virginia salt marshes.

Winter Foods of the Clapper Rail at Chincoteague, Virginia

The foregoing account pertained to foods of the clapper rail mainly during late summer and fall, when most of the birds were collected in the hunting season. In the more northern part of the winter range where fewer clapper rails occur, I was curious to find out what they fed on at that season in my main study area at Chincoteague. Common fiddler and square-backed fiddler crabs, major foods of the clapper at other seasons, are hibernating or in a state of torpor in their dens during most of the winter.

I spent two days in the Chincoteague salt marsh, January 29–30, 1984, and as expected did not see any fiddler crabs above ground. Temperatures were in the mid-30s to low 40s Fahrenheit. According to J. and M. Teal (1969), "Below 58° they [fiddlers] slow down very rapidly and quickly go into a torpor. When temperatures fall to those low limits, they retire into their burrows where they are safe from predators while they are in a slow-moving condition."

In studying 2 rails on separate winter territories, I discovered a number of freshly regurgitated pellets or castings, 40 of which I examined under a dissecting microscope. The pellets contained mostly fragments of common fiddler or square-backed fiddler crabs. On one occasion I flushed one of the rails from where it was feeding on a freshly killed square-backed fiddler. Thus it is evident that the clapper rails in the more northern part of their range, where fiddler crabs are mostly in a state of torpor in the winter, are able to extract or obtain in some way some of these crustaceans from their dens.

Although fiddler dens or burrows usually are deeper than the length of a clapper rail's bill, I have observed that when the ambient air temperature reaches 50° F., some fiddlers come up to the entrance of their dens. And at this temperature, when a clapper rail or a raccoon is working a fiddler colony, some crabs get curious because of the action or probing about their colony, and come up to the entrance of their dens or burrows, and this is apparently how some get caught. On one mild winter day on Chincoteague Island, I observed a raccoon catching square-backed fiddler crabs without digging for them. Another item found in several regurgitated clapper rail pellets were tiny mollusks, identified as the fat dove shell.

Richard W. Heard (1983) reviewed and compared the food habits of 5 subspecies of clapper rails endemic to the saltmarsh and mangrove swamps of the Atlantic and Gulf Coasts of the United States. He collected and examined 183 stomachs from these areas. His conclusion:

> Data from this and previous studies indicated that clapper rails are opportunistic omnivores, and occupy a relatively broad niche within tidal marsh ecosystems. A comparison of available data of the food of five clapper rail subspecies of the eastern United States indicates no distinct differences in their feeding behavior. Differences in the kinds of food eaten appear to simply reflect the types of marsh habitat (fresh, brackish, polyhaline) or geographical location (temperate, subtropical, tropical) in which a particular clapper rail population occurs.

Most of Heard's clapper rails were collected in the summer; and all of the northern clapper rails *(R. l. crepitans)* were collected at that season.

Foraging Behavior

In the brackish tidal marshes that border the Smyrna River near Delaware Bay, Delaware, at Taylor's Gut, I have found clapper and king rails foraging in the same tidal gut. An important food of the rails there is the red-jointed fiddler crab, *Uca minax* (Fig. 24), which is found farther upstream than other species of fiddler crabs in the Middle Atlantic states, but not far above the brackish zone, and as far as I am aware, not beyond tidewater in this area, which extends into the lower reaches of the freshwater marshes.

At Taylor's Gut, some of the tributaries are very narrow and have rather high embankments, up to 5 feet in height. The spartina marsh begins at this height and very near the top of the embankment. Just below the high tide mark near the top of the embankment are the holes or burrows of the fiddler crabs. The dens are inundated at high tide.

In stalking fiddlers at low tide, rails were often very slow and deliberate. When within striking distance, a rail would make a quick thrust or stab at a crab. But at high tide in summer at

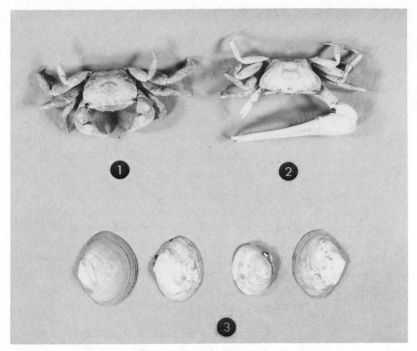

Fig. 24. Foods of clapper and king rails in brackish marsh at Taylor's Gut, Kent County, Delaware: (1) square-backed fiddler crab *(Sesarma reticulatum)*; (2) red-jointed fiddler crab *(Uca minax)*; (3) clam *(Macoma balthica)*. All 80% life-size. Photograph: Frederick C. Schmid.

Chincoteague, when water was 1 or 2 inches over fiddler burrows, I have seen a clapper rapidly move from one hole to another, quickly thrusting its bill in each hole.

When a fiddler is caught, it is often taken to some favorite feeding spot for dismembering, usually a pile of debris, and at Taylor's Gut, sometimes a muskrat house. The large claw of the male crab is sometimes disengaged in the following manner, as described by John Oney (1954): "The bird grasps the crab with its bill between the claw and the body. Then holding the crab, it vigorously shakes its head. The claw goes one way and the crab another. The bird then runs over and picks up the body and swallows it. The female crabs do not get the same treatment because both claws are nearly equal size." Most female fiddlers are small enough to be swallowed whole, and the same with the smaller males. Sometimes a large fiddler or a small blue crab is hacked to pieces and eaten bit by bit.

S. F. Pope, quoted in Bent's *Life Histories of North American Marsh Birds* (1926), provides some interesting notes on the clapper rail's dismantling of fiddler crabs in eastern Texas.

> On warm days the "fiddler" or fighting crabs would crawl out of their holes around the old schooner and were eagerly devoured by the rails. After catching one of the crabs they would usually remove the large claw before swallowing the victim. This was often accomplished with the assistance of a neighbor who would hold the crab in his beak while the other wrenched off the objectional limb; but this method was not always satisfactory to the bird that removed the claw, as the one that held the crab usually proceeded to bolt it while the other was left to hold the claw, or rather to drop it. On one occasion when crabs were not plentiful, a rail found and tackled an unusually large "fiddler," which it mauled around in the mud for some time without apparent effect. Suddenly, as if getting an idea, it left the crab and disappeared on the other side of the schooner, to return a moment later with a companion, the two soon disarming Mr. Crab. . . . Which one got the crab I can not say, as after scuffling over him, they disappeared from my sight in the tall grass.

In North Carolina, Adams and Quay (1958) noted that "on three occasions adult rails were seen to catch Fiddler Crabs and break them into smaller pieces. Chicks, following single file behind the parent, would then run up and eat the fragments."

Often a parent will wander 100 feet or more from its chicks in search of food for them. Upon catching a fiddler or some other item, it will then hurry to the nearest chick and deposit the food at its feet; or if the chick is old enough, it may grab the morsel from its parent's beak.

Occasionally a chick assumes a begging posture as its parent approaches with food. One 6- or 7-week-old chick still with a parent, but mostly foraging independently, would sometimes crouch close to the ground with its head drawn in and close to its body as its parent approached (Fig. 25). But the parent usually had no food for the chick and both would continue on, foraging independently. This chick would also assume the begging posture facing away from its parent. Such posturing may also have been in deference to its elder at that stage of the parent-chick relationship.

Fig. 25. Juvenile clapper rail crouching near parent when begging for food. It sometimes crouches facing away from its approaching parent, perhaps in deference to its elder at that stage of the juvenile-parent relationship. Illustration: John W. Taylor.

Regurgitated Pellets

The rail rejects most of the exoskeletal fragments of the fiddlers through the regurgitation of pellets. At Taylor's Gut, pellets contained fragments of the red-jointed fiddler crab and of the Baltic clam. As many as 14 pellets were found on a single muskrat house. At Chincoteague pellets were frequently found on boards carried out into the marsh by flood tides; and small pellets regurgitated by 2–3-day-old chicks were found in some nests.

Foods of the King Rail

Crustaceans are also a main food of the king rail. A series of stomachs examined from an interior location presents an interesting comparison. In the Grand Prairie rice-producing area near Stuttgart, Arkansas, domestic rice fields are a man-made marsh during late spring, summer, and early fall. Rice grows in 6 to 10 inches of water, and certian invertebrate and vertebrate animals and native plants characteristic of freshwater marshes occur there.

Waste grain and weed seeds in the stubble are available in the fall and winter.

In the rice field area, I collected and examined 118 king rail stomachs during the period 1950–1955. Animal life comprised 79 percent of the king rail's annual diet. The crayfish was the principal food, constituting 23 percent by volume of the annual diet. Aquatic insects were important foods, especially certain beetles and waterbugs. Aquatic beetles formed 14 percent of the annual food, and predaceous diving beetles furnished 19 percent of the winter diet. Like the clapper, king rails also like grasshoppers, which constituted 7 percent of their diet. Frogs accounted for 5 percent. Plant food comprised 21 percent of the annual diet, of which cultivated rice seed was 16 percent.

5.

COURTSHIP

Arrival on the Breeding Grounds and Calling

The red-winged blackbird, harbinger of spring on the coastal marsh, has been holding forth in song for about a month at Chincoteague, and many of the brant and a few snow geese are still on the bay and salt marsh when the first clapper rails begin their mating calls in late March and early April.

When we hear the first *kik-kik-kik-kik-kik-* or *bup-bup-bup-bup-bup-*, the mating call of the male, we can presume that this is a local bird, probably recently arrived from the South, because this call is given mainly on the breeding territory, or the section of marsh defended by the male. Little is known about the spring migration of the clapper rail, and it can be deduced, mainly by noting an increase in calling activity in the marsh, that there must have been some movement of populations along the coast.

Clapper rails migrate at night, but there seem to be no specific records of calling overhead as they move northward along the Middle Atlantic coast. Alexander Wilson, the pioneer ornithologist, reported in the early 1800s (1808–14) that in New Jersey the "coasters and fishermen often hear them on their migration in spring, generally a little before dawn."

About 75 miles north of Chincoteague, at Cape May, at the southern tip of New Jersey, Walker Hand (in Stone, *Bird Studies at Old Cape May*, 1937) stated that March 15 is the usual time for the spring arrival of the clapper rail. While he did not state so, he probably based his information on when he heard the first birds calling in the marsh. Bandings by biologists of the New Jersey Division of Fish, Game and Wildlife during the breeding season have shown that most clapper rails return to the same nesting area in subsequent years (Banding files, USFWS).

At dusk on April 2, 1984, I heard the mating calls of 6 clapper rails at Chincoteague, and the following day noted 2 mated pairs. It is conceivable that at least some pair bonds are formed by the last week in March. On the other hand, I noted at Chincoteague that there were a few unmated males on territories as late as the first week in June. I have observed that such unmated males are often in marginal or submarginal habitats. One richly colored adult male had a territory in a triangle between two roads. There was a small pond in the triangle, and the main vegetation bordering the pond was shrubs, namely hightide-bush *(Iva)*. Such shrubs are usually not clapper rail nesting habitat. Why this male would choose such a habitat when the area was surrounded by thousands of acres of prime salt marsh with plenty of unoccupied space for another adult male clapper rail was unknown.

The mating call of the clapper rail is similar to that of the king rail, and is given in the day and night. At Chincoteague it is heard most often from about the second week in April to the second week in May. On April 17, 1984, from one point where I was standing, in the 5-minute period 9:00–9:05 P.M. (EST) I counted 17 different clapper rails sounding the mating call.

The mating call continues to be used by the male to contact or rally the female after the pair bond is formed. Following the height of the nesting period in late May and early June at Chincoteague, it is heard less often.

Clapper rails have many different calls and, as already noted, the one usually associated with these birds and the one most often heard is the primary advertising call. It is given by both sexes. Often when this call is given by a single bird, it starts a chain reaction, and many rails may join in. The primary advertising call is also used by a member of a pair to rally or communicate with its mate; and when there is to be a changeover at the nest, one member of the pair calls its mate to replace it on the eggs.

In my studies of the king rail, I have recorded 18 different calls, the majority of which are given during the breeding season, and particularly during courtship and after the pair bond has been formed. I have heard at least 6 of these calls made by the clapper also, and there are probably many more. Such calls are generally the same in both species, except for variation in the primary advertising call (see Chapter 2).

The greatest number of different calls appears to be given after the pair bond has been formed and up to the beginning of nesting. Some of these calls are mostly subdued and are a means of communication between the pair. I have heard and seen one of a pair, usually the male, giving one such call, and then seen the female run to him. Sometimes during this period when the pair begin feeding close to one another and then gradually wander in opposite directions, becoming separated by 100 feet or so, one of the pair utters a subdued call and they return to feeding side by side. Some of the courtship and pair-bond notes are so subdued that a person has to be within 20 feet or less of the birds to hear them. One such call, given by both clapper and king rails, is a soft and rapid *tuk-tuk-tuk-*. I have heard the female uttering a soft *purr* or *churr*, like the *purr* of a cat. Several male clapper and king rails gave a deep booming sound requiring an effort which appeared to cause the body to expand slightly, and sounded something like *oom-oom-oom-*. The purpose of this "booming" call is not known. It was not vey loud and the females did not appear to be nearby when it was given. R. E. Stewart told me that he heard a clapper rail in a trap make this same sound.

In addition to the primary advertising call and mating and courtship calls there are various distress or alarm calls. One is a gutteral *rack-k-k-rack-k-k-*; another, *kik-kik-ker-r-r-r-*. Both calls are long and drawn out and may go on for several minutes. I have heard these calls when I flushed a rail from its nest. When I have flushed an adult with chicks, the disturbed bird uttered a sharp *gip-gip-gip-*, or *gep-gep-gep-*.

During the courtship and mating periods, the male often walks about with tail uplifted and with white undertail coverts extended or flashing. Sometimes when the male approached the female or vice versa, he would lower his tail to a horizontal position with white undertail coverts extended, pointing his slightly open bill toward the ground, slowly moving it from side to side in an arc of about 2 inches (Fig. 26). Another form of posturing occurs as the male, with neck stretched upward and bill open, approaches its mate, pursuing her for 2 or 3 feet. Both forms of posturing last for less than a minute, and end with the pair feeding together. Identical forms of posturing were noted in the king rail.

Fig. 26. Courtship display of male clapper rail. Its bill is slowly moved from side to side in an arc of about 2 inches. Illustration: John W. Taylor.

Pre-Nesting Behavior of a Pair of Clapper Rails at Chincoteague

On April 3 and 4, 1984, I spent 3 hours and 4 hours, respectively, observing a mated pair of clapper rails along the Chincoteague causeway. The pair spent most of its time in a territory along a roadside ditch and adjacent marsh edge that measured approximately 200 feet long and about 30 feet wide (another territory at Chincoteague was about 200 feet long by 40–50 feet wide). The causeway pair foraged back and forth from one end of the territory to the other. On at least 3 occasions within 1 hour on April 4, the male wandered over to a pile of dead *Spartina* stems that had been washed up on the edge of the roadside ditch from a recent flood tide. He had pushed up some of the *Spartina* stems as if to fashion a shell of a nest including a dome. On one occasion he remained concealed in the nest shell for 10 minutes, and on another, 8 minutes. While there he uttered a soft *tuk-tuk-tuk-*, barely audible at 10 feet, where I was stationed in an automobile. From time to time the male would pick up a few materials just outside the structure and carry them inside. On one occasion when at the nest site the male gave the mating call (*kik-kik-*) and the female, standing about 30 feet away, answered with a similar call, and ran over to join her mate. This is the first and only time I have heard the female uttering the mating call.

I concluded that the male's action was a case of symbolic nest-building, a part of the courtship ritual, as a later inspection of the site showed no further work by the bird(s). The true nest, with 8 eggs, was located on May 16 approximately 60 feet away in typical saltmarsh cordgrass habitat.

Symbolic nest-building was observed in the king rail at Stuttgart, Arkansas. In this case a male was observed carrying nesting material into a hole in a rice field dike through which water was draining from the field into a roadside ditch. The dike was about 2½ feet in height, and the hole was large enough for the bird to pass easily from one side of the dike to the other. The light stream of water did not prevent an accumulation of a few pieces of nesting material. However, the nest was not completed. Two days later the true nest was started about 10 yards from the hole in the dike.

Courtship Feeding

Courtship feeding was observed at Taylor's Gut, Delaware, when a male clapper rail presented a red-jointed fiddler crab to its mate, and at Chincoteague, Virginia, where a common fiddler crab was used for the same purpose. Similar behavior was observed near Stuttgart, Arkansas, where during a 2-hour period a male king rail was seen to capture 7 crayfish, 5 of which were presented to his mate.

Courtship feeding continues during the incubation period. In early June 1983 at Chincoteague, I watched a male clapper rail make 5 trips to obtain fiddler crabs to be presented to his incubating mate. During a half-hour period, he swam across a tidal gut that was approximately 100 feet wide, and returned to his mate with the morsel. Once while looking for a fiddler he flushed a moth, which he caught and took back to his mate.

6.

NESTING

The Nesting Season

The nesting season along the Atlantic Coast varies with latitude. Published records indicate that nesting begins in late March in the South Atlantic area (Florida, Georgia, South Carolina), and about a month later along the Virginia and New Jersey coasts. An early date at Nassau County, Long Island, is April 11, 1965 (E. Mac-Namara, in R. W. Johnson, 1965–66); and at Cape May, New Jersey, April 14, 1903 (Walker Hand, in Stone, 1937). At Chincoteague, an early nest with eggs was noted on April 17, but most nesting is not underway there until mid-May. The height of the nesting season at Chincoteague is the last week in May and the first week in June, when most nests have full clutches, and some eggs are beginning to hatch; and the height of the nesting season in coastal New Jersey is the first week in June (Kozicky and Schmidt, 1949; Widjeskog and Shoemaker, 1982).

Second nesting attempts at Chincoteague occur mostly in the last two weeks of June, and a few late nestings may take place in July and early August. An unusually late date for a number of nests was reported by M. A. Byrd, Gary Seek, and Bill Smith (1971), who found 16 nests in Gull Marsh near Cobb Island, Virginia, on July 23, 1971; and R. E. Stewart (1951b) lists August 10, 1951, for the latest date of 4 nests with eggs at Cobb Island. A late nesting record for Nassau County, Long Island, is August 4, 1965 (Johnson, 1965–66). Young produced from such late-July and August nestings would not reach flight age until at least mid-September.

Nesting Density

On the Atlantic Coast, clapper rail breeding population density studies have been made in New Jersey, Virginia, South Carolina, Georgia, and possibly other areas. Such determinations were made by counts of active nests or call counts during the breeding season. Areas for nest counts or censusing were apparently selected because of expected high populations.

At Chincoteague, May 25–June 9, 1950, R. E. Stewart (1951a) made a survey of nesting populations in a 47-acre tract in an area bordering Wire Narrows (Fig. 27). The vegetation was mostly *Spartina alterniflora*. A total of 79 nests were located in the tract, and most were in the tall-growth cordgrass, usually within 15 feet of a tidal gut. The following year, Stewart found the nesting population in the same tract down by 40 percent (1951b). It is important to note that no more than 50 percent of the 47-acre tract had optimum nesting cover. Away from the tidal guts, in the central part of the tract, much of the vegetation is too short for such cover.

Thirty-one years later, during the last week in May 1981, my wife Anna and I, using Stewart's map, surveyed the same Wire Narrows tract, and found only 22 nests; and the following year, 1982, only 19. But during the first week in June 1984, we located 36 nests.

The only noticeable difference in the 47-acre tract between the time of Stewart's survey and ours was the presence of nesting laughing gulls in the 1980s and none in 1950 and 1951. Most of the 135 active gull nests in 1981 (105 in 1982, and 45 in 1984) were in the same narrow band of cordgrass bordering the tidal guts where

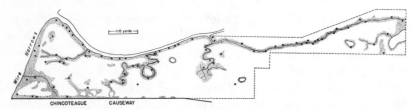

Fig. 27. Map of R. E. Stewart's 1950 study area at Chincoteague, Virginia, showing distribution of occupied clapper rail nests. The nest locations are shown by the large dots while the tall growth of saltmarsh cordgrass is represented by the stippled areas. Clapper rail nests were censused in this same tract by the author in 1981, 1982, and 1984. Illustration courtesy of R. E. Stewart and Wildlife Management Institute.

the clappers nested (Fig. 28). Several of the clapper nests were only 3 or 4 feet from laughing gull nests. There was no evidence of predation on rail eggs. There would be no competition for nest sites, as there was ample additional typical habitat unused by both rails and gulls. Perhaps the many gulls may have an intimidating effect on rails that nest in gull colonies. On the far northern breeding grounds of the snow goose, Paul Johnsgard (1979) noted that where the geese and herring gulls nest within a few yards of each other, "the goose is curiously immune to predation by the gull. Apparently the gull's predatory tendencies are inhibited within its own nesting territory; the presence of the gull thus confers upon the goose a degree of protection from other nest predators." In one section of the 47-acre tract at Chincoteague, an active clapper rail nest was surrounded by a small colony of 12 nests of Forster's terns. Terns are extremely protective of their nesting colonies, and it is a fortunate clapper rail that nests among them.

In 1948, in the Ocean City, Cape May County, area of New Jersey, E. L. Kozicky and F. V. Schmidt (1949) located 43 clapper rail nests in 372 acres of saltmarsh cordgrass.

The highest density of territorial males in the Chincoteague area that I noted in 1984, based on mating calls, was 4 pairs per acre in a 10-acre tract. In South Carolina in 1963, Warren Blandin (1965) had approximately 4 pairs in one of his 10-acre study plots (see Table 3). Using a call-counting technique during the mating season, Robert E. Mangold (1974) was able to establish an index of abundance for clapper rails in several New Jersey salt marshes (see Table 4).

Table 3. Breeding Densities (Pairs) in Beaufort, S.C., Study Areas (Blandin, 1965)

	1960	1961	1962	1963	1964
Albergotti Creek (10 acres)	11	32	30	39	28
Chowan Creek (15 acres)	10	18	18	32	38

Table 4. Breeding Densities (Pairs) at Tuckerton, N.J., Study Areas (Mangold, 1974)

	1969	1970	1971	1972	1973
Hatfield area (92 acres)	26	33	35	40	40
Drag Sedge area (30 acres)	10	18	19-20	21	17

Fig. 28. Nest and eggs of laughing gull beside tidal gut at low tide, Chincoteague, Virginia, June 3, 1977. Clapper rail nests are placed in this same marsh edge habitat.

The Nest

Most nests at Chincoteague and elsewhere along the coast are placed in a medium-growth type of saltmarsh cordgrass, usually close to a tidal gut (Fig. 29). Such an optimum growth for nesting is about 3 or 4 feet high. In some sections, particularly in South Carolina and Georgia coastal marshes, the saltmarsh cordgrass closest to the tidal gut reaches a height of 6 feet. Clappers seldom use such tall stands in which to build their nests. A medium-growth saltmarsh cordgrass fringes some of the tidal pools out in the body of the marsh and is also utilized for nesting. The salt-meadow cordgrass, a dense, short-growth, wind-blown form farther back in the marsh, is seldom used for nesting at Chincoteague. However, in wandering among heron-egret-ibis nesting colonies I have occasionally flushed an incubating clapper from a small patch of saltmeadow. The needlerush or blackrush marsh, usually growing at a slightly higher and drier elevation, is a minor type for nesting, although in South Carolina, Blandin (1965b) found a number of nests in this habitat.

R. W. Johnson (1965–66) reported that in Nassau County, Long Island, clappers commonly nest in some mixture of saltmeadow cordgrass, saltmarsh cordgrass, saltgrass, and hightide-bush. An unusual nesting site in South Carolina was a 15-foot-high sand dune, 200 feet from water (Troup D. Perry, in Bent, 1926). Also in South Carolina, Blandin noted that two birds renested in the abandoned nests of other clapper rails (1965a).

At the Wire Narrows marsh near Chincoteague in May 1981, nests (21) were placed on an average of 5 feet from the edge of a tidal gut—one as close as 2 feet, another as far away as 12 feet. In another area where the band of tall saltmarsh cordgrass was wider, a nest was 40 feet from the gut; and in 1984, I found a nest 300 feet from the nearest tidal gut. In Cape May County, New Jersey, Kozicky and Schmidt (1949) reported that 45 of 63 nests were located within 12 feet of a tidal gut or a mosquito ditch. Some nests were as close as 30 feet apart (see Fig. 27).

Most clapper rail nests are placed in a uniform stand of saltmarsh cordgrass. The nest canopy or dome slightly disrupts the uniform pattern of the vegetation, revealing the location to a person looking for nests (Fig. 30). However, the canopy over most nests often shields the eggs from avian predators such as the fish

Fig. 29. Location of clapper rail nest in relation to tidal gut, Chincoteague, Virginia, in May.

Fig. 30. Dome or canopy over clapper rail's nest helps to conceal the eggs from such avian predators as the fish crow.

crow hunting over the marsh. I have been able to spot some canopies at 50 feet.

At Chincoteague, the nest platform or cup holding the eggs is usually constructed about 1 foot above normal high tide level. The diameter of the platform is about 8–10 inches, and the canopy is about 1 foot above the platform. Nests usually have a runway or ramp leading to the platform. If high tide is a little above normal and begins to flood the nest, the incubating bird will raise the level of the platform by tucking grass beneath the eggs.

The response of nesting clapper rails to rising water was observed by J. A. Jackson (1983) at a nest at Ocean Springs, Jackson Couty, Mississippi, on April 13, 1980:

> Within 24 hrs. more than 20cm of rain fell in the area. When the rails were first observed at 09:30 it had just stopped raining. One rail was at the nest, a second judged to be the male by its brighter orange bill and more distinctive flank and head markings, was hurriedly adding material to the nest. I watched for 75 min as the male worked—at first hardly leaving the nest to get material, but later moving more than a meter away. He put everything into his efforts, using wings to balance himself, bracing with his feet against the *Spartina* as he tugged at the

brown stems, almost flipping over backwards as he rushed material to
the nest or to the incubating female. The female moved only to tuck
bits under her and to rearrange material around the nest. During a
3-min period the male made 17 trips to the nest. This rate was
maintained for over an hour, and then when it started to rain again,
the male's pace seemed to quicken.

The female was still incubating on April 21.

I have observed this same adaptive response in king rails. I
quote from my monograph (1969) on that species:

> After a heavy rain on the Arkansas Grand Prairie, an incubating rail
> was observed working rapidly to build up its cattail nest above the
> rising water in a roadside ditch. By reaching out with its bill all around
> the nest and picking up materials (mostly cattail leaf fragments),
> which it tucked beneath the eggs, and by using most of the canopy for
> the same purpose, the bird managed to keep the eggs about 2 inches
> above the rising water. The ditch was nearly dry before the rain, and
> the eggs were then 5 inches from the ground. At peak depth, the water
> was 21 inches deep. On another occasion a nest with eggs 2½ inches
> from the ground was located in a rice field that had been temporarily
> drained. The next day, the field was flooded to a depth of 5 inches, and
> the eggs were raised to 7 inches from the ground. As the water
> continued to rise, the incubating bird persisted in elevating the eggs
> by tucking rice leaves from the canopy under them.

In the king rail, the male takes the more active role in nest
building. From the above account by Jackson, and from my own
observations, apparently the same can be said of the male clapper.

The nest of the clapper rail is not always completed before the
first egg is laid. As noted by Walter Hoxie (1887) at Frogmore,
South Carolina: "The first time I found the nest it contained only
one egg, and did not seem wide enough to hold more than one
more. . . . As each new egg was laid they added fresh material to the
outside, until the nest was at least amply sufficient to contain the
full set of eight."

I have also noted nests of the closely related king rail still
under construction at the onset of egg laying. Near Stuttgart,
Arkansas, I observed a bird building a nest on the side of a small
bank next to a wet ditch. The bird was pulling in grass to form the
sides and canopy for the nest. The next morning I found that
construction was still in the initial stage, but 2 eggs had been laid
on the bare ground and were surrounded by just a few dead plant

fragments. A purple gallinule, which builds a nest like the clapper rail, was reported by Sam Grimes (1944) to have a nest platform 6 inches thick when the first egg was laid. As the eggs began to hatch, the nest was built up until the platform was 13 inches thick.

Clutch Size

The average clutch size along the Atlantic Coast ranges from about 8 to 10 eggs (Fig. 31). Clutches of 13 and 14 eggs are relatively uncommon. Walker Hand (Stone, 1937) found a nest at Cape May, New Jersey, containing 20 eggs—probably the work of more than one female. Such "dumps nests" are not uncommon among some species of waterfowl, and I have noted such in the purple gallinule, another rallid, in the Louisiana rice fields (Fig. 32).

The size of completed clutches was detemined for 149 first nests at Chincoteague, 1950–1953 (Stewart and Meanley, 1960). The number of nests for each clutch size was:

4 eggs	1 nest	(0.7%)
5 eggs	4 nests	(2.7%)
6 eggs	5 nests	(3.4%)
7 eggs	13 nests	(8.7%)
8 eggs	22 nests	(14.7%)
9 eggs	43 nests	(28.9%)
10 eggs	39 nests	(26.2%)
11 eggs	21 nests	(14.1%)
12 eggs	1 nest	(0.7%)
Total	149 nests	(100.0%)

Nests with 9 eggs represented the largest clutch-size class, closely followed by those with 10 eggs. The mean clutch size was 9.00 ± 0.19 eggs.

In New Jersey, "the average number of eggs per clutch in 1948, 1949, and 1950 was 9.9, 10.0 and 9.3 respectively, based on 176 completed clutches" (Schmidt and McLain, 1951); and in Nassau County, Long Island, New York, in 1965, clutch size in 35 nests was 9.2 eggs, and in 1966 in 43 nests, 9.0 eggs (Johnson, 1965–1966). The average clutch size for 140 first nests in Beaufort County, South Carolina, 1960–1964, was 8.7 eggs (Blandin, 1965b).

Since the height of the season along the Virginia coast is the last week in May and the first week in June, it is reasonable to assume that the 13 nests found by Stewart and Meanley (1960) June

Fig. 31. Nest and eggs of marsh hen in salt marsh, Chincoteague, Virginia, in June.

20–27, 1959, and 3 nests found on August 10, 1951, represented second clutches following destruction of the first nest or following a successful first nest. The mean clutch size of this series was 5.62 ± 1.06, which is 3.38 less than the mean for the first or primary Virginia nests. This difference can be considered to be statistically significant. The number of second nests for each clutch size was:

3 eggs	1 nest	(6.2%)
4 eggs	2 nests	(12.5%)
5 eggs	5 nests	(31.2%)
6 eggs	5 nests	(31.2%)
7 eggs	1 nests	(6.2%)
8 eggs	1 nests	(6.2%)
9 eggs	1 nests	(6.2%)
Total	16 nests	(100.0%)

Egg Laying, Incubation, and Hatching

Kozicky and Schmidt (1949) reported that the rate of laying in 4 New Jersey nests was about 1 egg a day. "The history of the four nests was as follows: seven eggs in eight days, five in five, eight in eight, and 11 in 15." In some nests, particularly those with larger

Fig. 32. Dump nest (eggs laid by more than one bird) of 14 eggs of purple gallinule, a member of the rail family, in domestic rice field at Mamou, Evangeline Parish, Louisiana, 1956. Normal clutch is usually 6–8 eggs, occasionally 10 eggs.

clutches, incubation begins before the clutch is complete, thus a clutch may hatch over an extended period, often several days.

An Arkansas king rail nest was under daily observation from the time the first egg was laid on April 1, until the last egg hatched on May 4. Eleven eggs comprised the complete clutch, and incubation started with the laying of the tenth egg on April 10. In a Long Island sora (rail) nest of 10 eggs, Greenlaw and Miller (1983) reported that 1 egg was laid each day, and incubation began with the laying of the fourth egg.

At 6 nests in New Jersey, Kozicky and Schmidt reported that the incubation period was about 20 days, with extremes of 18 and 22 days. The incubation period at 4 Arkansas king rail nests was 21 days, 22 days, 22 or 23 days, and approximately 23 days.

Schmidt and McLain (1951) noted that the clapper rail lays its eggs before 8:00 A.M. In Arkansas, king rail eggs were laid between 7:00 P.M. and 7:00 A.M.

Both sexes take turns incubating (Fig. 33). This was demonstrated by John Oney (1954) in Georgia, who sprayed an incubating bird with a bright color paint, and the following day there was an unpainted bird sitting on the clutch. I demonstrated this technique with the king rail in the Arkansas rice fields with the same results. I also have witnessed an exchange at the nest by both sexes of clapper and king rails.

As stated, the hatching of a clutch may take several days. In their New Jersey study, Kozicky and Schmidt found that the chicks usually pipped about 48 hours before hatching, and the clutch required from 24 to 48 hours to complete hatching. At Chincoteague, I observed that the first chick of a 10-egg clutch had just hatched and was still wet at 7:30 P.M., June 4. At 8:30 A.M., June 6, the ninth was the last egg to be hatched. The tenth egg was infertile. Thus, the clutch hatched over a period of 37 hours. A king rail clutch at Stuttgart, Arkansas, took approximately 55 hours from the time the first egg was pipped until the clutch of 10 eggs hatched. Hatched eggshells are either removed from the nest, or are eaten by the adults, or disintegrate and filter down into the base of the nest.

Renesting and Double Broods

Schmidt and McLain (1951) in New Jersey and Blandin (1963) in South Carolina were able to determine through banding or tagging

Fig. 33. Changeover at the nest. Both sexes take turns incubating the eggs. Chincoteague, Virginia, June 7, 1983. Photograph: Luther C. Goldman.

nesting birds that some clapper rails renest or have a second nest, and some have more than one successful brood.

At Beaufort, South Carolina, Blandin used yellow tags with black numbers attached to the backs of nest-trapped birds to determine if there was a second nesting attempt after an initial failure or a successful first hatch. Of 69 birds marked with back tags and banded, 40 were not seen again, and the remaining 29 were observed 228 times. Of these 29, 13 were known to renest.

Nine of Blandin's marked birds renested one time, 2 renested twice, 1 renested 3 times, and 1 (#5) renested 5 times. "Seven of the 9 birds (77.7 per cent) that renested once hatched a brood. One of 2 birds (50.0 per cent) renesting twice hatched a brood, and the bird renesting 3 times was unsuccessful on its third renesting attempt. Bird #5 built a first nest, 5 renests and an additional nest in which no eggs were laid. This individual failed to hatch a clutch." Blandin determined that at least 7 marked birds produced 2 successful broods.

In Blandin's study, second or renest sites were located on an average of about 100 feet from the initial nests. Some, however, were much closer. In one case the same nest was used.

Nesting Success

As far as I can ascertain, the following observations pertain to the period of initial nesting attempts. A nest was considered successful if at least 1 egg hatched. Unless a nest is destroyed by flooding or a predator, most of the eggs in a clutch will hatch. Occasionally a last unhatched egg is deserted, one of the eggs is infertile, or a chick dies in the process of hatching.

At Chincoteague in 1950, Stewart (1951a) found nesting success to be about 90 percent in his study area. "The hatching success of the 79 nests was very high, eggs of only 5 nests (6 percent) being definitely known to have been destroyed." This success is similar to the findings of Kozicky and Schmidt (1949) in Cape May County, New Jersey, in 1948, who reported that 89.3 percent of the nests in their study area hatched successfully (50 of 56 nests). "In the 50 successful nests, a total of 513 eggs were laid; however, only 448 eggs (87.3 per cent) hatched." In the same area, Schmidt and Mc-Lain (1951) reported nesting success in 1949 at 94 percent, and in 1950 at 69 percent. In more recent studies in Ocean County, New Jersey, Mangold (1974) and Widjeskog and Shoemaker (1983) found nesting success comparatively high, as in the earlier studies in that state (see Table 5).

**Table 5. Clapper Rail Nesting and Hatching Success for 1980–83
on Ocean County, New Jersey, Study Areas***

Year	Number of Nests	Success-ful Nests	Number of Eggs	Success-ful Eggs	Average Number Eggs per Nest	Nesting Success %	Hatching Success %
1980	17	17	151	149	8.9	100	98.6
1981	6	5	55	45	9.2	83.3	81.8
1982	7	6	68	67	9.7	87.8	98.5
1983	10	8	80	69	8.6	80.0	86.3

In the 5-year period 1960–1964, in Beaufort County, South Carolina, Blandin (1965b) reported a 36.9 percent nesting success in 260 nests. Nesting success varied from a high of 60.0 percent in 1961 to a low of 16.7 percent in 1964. Nesting success was also low

*from Widjeskog and Shoemaker, 1983

in a 1956 North Carolina study, with only 11 of 26 nests (42 percent) successful (Adams and Quay, 1958).

I suspect that the high rate of success in New Jersey and at Chincoteague may be due to the more isolated locations of the two study areas from the mainland. The study area at Chincoteague is a marsh bordering the four-mile-long causeway leading from the mainland to Chincoteague Island. Raccoons can follow the causeway to the bordering marshes, but in the many days over the years that I did field work in rail-nesting marshes bordering the causeway I never saw signs of raccoons nor any dead ones on the road.

Fish crows course the Chincoteague causeway marshes, but I believe that the local colony of nesting laughing gulls is a buffer for the clapper rail, as the open nests of the gulls are easily found compared to the fairly well hidden nests of the clapper. A duck blind in the marsh used by the crows as a feeding station was surrounded by broken gull eggs, but none of the clapper. In New Jersey, Mangold reported that a rail clutch was hatched in a nest located less than 25 feet from a power pole on which a pair of fish crows had an active nest. However, it is well known that in some areas fish crows destroy many clapper rail eggs. Perhaps in such areas there are no nesting buffer species such as gulls, terns, oyster-catchers, herons, and egrets close by (see Chapter 11).

Nesting success varies widely from place to place and from year to year. In areas where raccoons prowl the marsh or where there has been a spring or flood tide, the number of successful nests will be lower.

Survival of Young

Apparently very little effort has been made to determine the survival rate of juvenile clapper rails. In South Carolina, Blandin (1965a) says, "Observations of known broods indicate that juvenile mortality may be as high as 66 percent and is generally more than 50 per cent (6 broods)."

During the period July 15–17, 1984, I saw 9 broods of clapper rail chicks at Chincoteague (Table 6). Some of the chicks were less than 1 month old, thus were probably from renesting or second nesting attempts, as the average time for first complete clutches at Chincoteague is the last week in May through the first week in June. Clutch size of renesting or second nesting attempts is smaller than first attempts.

**Table 6. Clapper Rail Brood Size at Chincoteague, Virginia,
July 15–17, 1984**

Number Chicks in Brood	Approximate Age	Approximate Date of Hatching
2	5–6 weeks	June 1
2	5–6 weeks	June 1
4	4 weeks	June 15
6	2 weeks	July1
2	3 weeks	June 25
7	2–3 weeks	June 25–July 1
4	2 weeks	July 1
3	6 weeks	June 1
4	1 week	July 10

During the period July 18 to August 31, 1951, at Chincoteague, R. E. Stewart (1951b) banded 742 clapper rails. Of this total, 68 (about 11 percent) were adults and 674 (89 percent) were juveniles or immatures. This may not be a true picture of the young:adult ratio during this period of the summer—adults more readily avoid being trapped. On numerous occasions I have come upon traps with a brood of chicks inside and one or both parents standing on the outside. Also the ratio probably changes as the summer progresses into fall, because the young of the year would be more vulnerable to predation, hunting, and the hazards of their first southward migration.

At Beaufort and Southport, North Carolina, Adams and Quay (1958) obtained information on age ratios of summer-trapped birds and of fall- and winter-shot birds (Table 7). The summer-trapped birds in this sample would seem to be near an expected age ratio at this season (4.9:1); but, in contrast to Stewart's trapping results, the sample is much smaller.

Table 7. Age Ratios of Clapper Rails in North Carolina and Virginia

Beaufort and Southport, N.C., 1955–56 (Adams and Quay, 1958)			
Summer:	212 birds	(176 juveniles, 36 adults)	4.9:1
Fall:	263 birds	(139 immatures, 24 adults)	5.8:1
Fall–Winter:	42 birds	(35 immatures, 7 adults)	5.0:1

Accomack County, Va., 1983 (author)			
September:	80 birds	(60 immatures, 20 adults)	3.0:1

7.

THE BROOD SEASON

Parental Care and Development of Young

Both parents attend the chicks in the early stages of development. In their North Carolina study, Adams and Quay (1958) stated that "while one parent brooded newly hatched chicks and incubated any remaining eggs, the other sometimes led the first-hatched chicks as far as 50 feet away from the nest."

At an Arkansas nest of a king rail, the parents alternately participated in incubating remaining eggs and brooding newly hatched chicks. Toward the end of the hatching period the non-brooding parent was observed within 25 feet of the nest with several of the chicks. In one case, a pair of king rails, one of which was marked, and their three-day-old chicks spent most of the day within 20 yards of the nest; and 19 days later were seen only 10 yards from the nest.

The parents sometimes construct several brood nests near the main nest, and one of them is used during parts of the day and at night. The brood nests are mainly platforms with no canopy.

Adams and Quay state that "the parental-care period extended into the fifth or sixth week after hatching. When chicks less than five weeks old were in traps, the parent birds were usually nearby. . . . In no case of trapped chicks more than six weeks old was either parent believed to be in attendance."

An interesting observation was made by Mangold in New Jersey when he was trapping and banding clapper rails. "Whenever an adult with brood was captured, the adult was invariably a male." This would seem to indicate that the female was on a second nest.

An adult traveling with chicks that are only a few days old utters soft notes somewhat resembling the *cluck* of a barnyard hen, but sounding more like *woof, woof, woof-*.

From my observations, it takes the precocial young rail chick at least 1 hour after hatching to move out of the nest if it chooses to do so, or if frightened. The egg tooth is lost between the fourth and sixth days.

The newly hatched chick is covered with a coal-black down (Fig. 34). The bill has a pied pattern. The natal black down is present during most of the first month, but by the fourth week there is the first evidence of juvenal plumage—tufts of white about the ear (auriculars) and tufts of white on ventral feather tracts or underparts (Fig. 35). By the end of the fifth week, quills begin to appear in some birds; at about 60 days, the immature plumage has mostly replaced the black down. By the ninth or tenth week the young rail is attempting to fly, and by this time the young bird rather resembles the adult, except for the duller color of the legs and bill. Adams and Quay note that at 6 to 9 weeks the iris is olive-drab, but by the tenth week, the iris is becoming orange-brown.

Fig. 34. Newly hatched clapper rail chicks.

R. E. Stewart (1965b) notes that in August, "the larger young may be distinguished from adults by the following characters: olive-green iris instead or orange or orange-brown; bill pinkish-gray instead of orange-tinged; legs blackish instead of flesh-colored; much less buffy coloration on the breast. Iris begins to change color about the time that the plumage of young is fully developed—at this time appearing olive-brown."

Adams & Quay state that "by the time the young birds are fully feathered and flying [9–10 weeks], their calls were like those of adults." The first evidence of one of my captive clappers making the primary advertising call of an adult was at 6 months of age.

Notes on Clapper Rail Broods at Chincoteague

During the period July 18–20, 1983, I had an opportunity to observe several adult clapper rails with broods at Chincoteague. One family group was composed of an adult and 3 young approximately 6 weeks of age; another, adults with 4 downy chicks about 1 week old. I estimated the ages of the young clappers from my experience

Fig. 35. One-month-old king rail chick. A clapper rail chick of the same age has a similar appearance.

in raising clapper rails in captivity from the newly hatched chick to maturity.

The family with older young was kept under almost constant observation for 3 hours on July 18, as they foraged during a high-tide period in a narrow ditch close to the causeway leading to Chincoteague. The water in the ditch was 6 to 8 inches in depth.

This was a period when the young were becoming independent, one of them foraging on its own, often as much as 200 feet from its parent. Two of the three young followed the parent closely except when it foraged, completely exposed, in the middle of the ditch, at which time they moved along the marsh edge. When the parent stopped to bathe and preen in the middle of the ditch, the young would stand about 4 feet away, partly concealed at the edge of the marsh, watching. The parent would preen for 6 to 9 minutes following a bath.

The ditch was pocked with fiddler crab burrows. The adult bird often foraged rapidly, poking its bill into one hole after another. One of the young stood motionless by a fiddler burrow for 8 minutes, presumably hoping for a crab to appear.

Once when one of the young was separated from its parent, it noticed a black duck feeding about 30 feet away in the same ditch. The young rail, probably mistaking the duck for its parent, ran toward the duck. But, when about 15 feet away, it quickly turned around and ran into the marsh. Shortly thereafter, the adult rail was standing and preening in the ditch, and did not move as the duck foraged within 3 feet of it.

The following day, July 19, at high tide, presumably the same adult and 3 young were in the same section of the ditch. This time only one of the young rails was following its parent begging for food; the other two were foraging independently, at times 50 feet away. The adult with these approximately six-week-old young was not heard to utter any sound when the family was within close range of this observer; but the young uttered a soft *chitty-chitty-chitty-* when near their parent.

On July 20, the pair of adults with week-old downy chicks were noted in a narrow band of saltmarsh cordgrass next to a tidal gut that was about 100 feet wide. The adults endeavored to coax the chicks to swim across the gut to the extensive marsh on the opposite side. Twice, as I watched, both adults swam approximately halfway across the gut, then turned around in midstream to see if the chicks were following. The chicks would not follow, so the adults returned to the narrow band of cover where the chicks were waiting for them. Although chicks of that early age can swim, it may have been the width of the tidal gut or the presence of many noisy adult and juvenile laughing gulls nearby that frightened them.

About a quarter of a mile away from where the above observations were made, I found 2 dead clapper rail chicks, 2 to 3 weeks old, in what had been a nesting colony of laughing gulls, and where many young gulls were assembled to be fed. The clapper chick carcasses were among many shells of crustaceans, one of the types of food fed to the young gulls.

8.

MOLTING AND THE POST-BREEDING SEASON

During the later stages of the breeding season and following it, adult clapper rails undergo a complete postnuptial molt, during which time they are flightless for about a month. The remiges and rectrices (wing and tail feathers) are shed simultaneously. Unlike waterfowl (ducks, geese, and swans) which are also flightless for about a month, rails are less handicapped, as they live in dense cover and fly very little at any time except during migration.

The contour or body feathers begin molting first, with the remiges and rectrices following. The young or juvenile undergoes a partial molt that does not include a replacement of the wing and tail feathers. Several young birds trapped in Delaware were beginning their postjuvenal molt at the time the flight feathers were developing and about half unsheathed.

The molting period of clapper rails in the Middle Atlantic states extends from about late June into early October, with most birds molting in July and August. I collected a pair of clapper rails at Woodland Beach, Delaware, on June 29, 1964, that were replacing their body feathers.

In the course of his banding operations at Chincoteague, Virginia, R. E. Stewart (1951) made the following notes on clapper rail molt:

> During the trapping period (July 16–August 31) most of the adults were undergoing their post-nuptial molt. . . . The individual molting period lasts about one month. The first adult observed in full molt was trapped on July 21. During the period August 24 to August 31 (period just before the hunting season) a total of 11 adults were trapped. Of these only 5 had completed their molt and were capable of flight, while 4 were in heavy molt, and were completely flightless.

Surprisingly enough the other two adults had not even started to molt and were in very worn plumage.

On August 3, 1967, I collected 2 adult king rails from the Nanticoke River marshes near Vienna, Maryland, that had not yet begun to molt. The period of molting of clapper and king rails is about the same.

H. C. Oberholser (1937) states that the first winter plumage (of young of the year) is completely developed sometime between late August and November. At Chincoteague, the main hatching period is usually during the first 2 weeks in June, thus most juvenile rails have completed their molt by late August or early September. With the renesting of some adult birds in late June and a few records of nesting in July to mid-August, a few young would be completing their molt well into October. I collected a young clapper rail near Townsend, Virginia, on September 28, 1983, that could not yet fly.

During the molting period, particularly when they have shed their flight feathers, clapper rails appear to be more retiring in their habits. They expose themselves less in open areas, i.e., they do not seem to appear on the mud flats as much as during the nesting season; nor do they seem to swim across the tidal guts so much as earlier in the summer and in the spring. Their mobility has been curtailed somewhat. Waterfowl adapt to this flightless period similarly, as indicated by Welty in *The Life of Birds* (1975): "They compensate for the hazards of flightlessness by retreating to isolated bodies of water where they can find food and escape enemies by swimming on and under the water. Huge flocks of ducks, geese, and swans commonly undertake special molt migrations whereby they seek sheltered retreats for the safe renewal of their flight feathers." And, as Albert Hochbaum (1944) says, many songbirds "remain solitary near the breeding territory, quietly inconspicuous during the molt, but announcing their presence in late August with autumnal song."

Also at this season, some clappers appear to be territorial. Although they weren't marked, I saw several clappers in the same places where I found them nesting in May and June. I saw them in these areas in early September during the day and heard calling there at night. During the first and last week in September 1983 at Chincoteague, I observed an adult and nearly full-grown immatures in the same quarter-acre area. Their territory was an isolated small patch of saltmarsh cordgrass lying between 2 roads. They were seen on that territory daily during the 2 weeks of my observations that month.

Roth and several others noted the movements of clapper rails in Louisiana marshes in their radio telemetry study in which they attached transmitters to the backs of 12 birds. The period of contact with these birds ranged from 7 to 47 days. Results of the radio telemetry study indicated that during the summer, Louisiana clapper rails had an average minimum home range of 168 yards along canals and tidal ditches, and average daily movements of 58 yards.

Toward the end of the molting period, in the first week in September, clappers seem to be as abundant on the Eastern Shore of Virginia marshes as during the breeding season. There is very little calling during hot sunny days when the temperatures reach the mid-90s. During a 24-hour period there may be more calling at night. On September 8, 1983, I was on the Chincoteague marsh during the day for 6 hours and heard clappers calling only 11 times. The night before, at 9:30 P.M. (EDT), I heard 28 calling clappers after one bird started the chain of calls. (Birds answered from different parts of the marsh so it was possible to count the number of calls.)

While the clapper rail population at Chincoteague appears to be as abundant in early September as in early summer, there have been some marked changes in other bird populations. The estimated 5,000 pairs of adult laughing gulls and their offspring, which were in the same marsh during the breeding season with nesting clappers, began to depart from the area in August. There were still numerous snowy and great egrets, and Louisiana herons, which nested nearby, but the local breeding glossy ibis population that nested with the herons and egrets had left the area.

Late August and early September is the height of the southward shorebird migration in the area. The black-bellied plover, called "bullhead" in years past when they were hunted, and the lesser yellowlegs were the most vociferous shorebirds in the salt marsh during this period. Boat-tailed grackles which are present the year around occur throughout the salt marsh and are still molting. Most of them are bobtailed, and some are almost tailless and just beginning to grow new tails.

The raptors or predatory birds are beginning to show up; some will be migrating through and some may be staying over the winter. A few marsh hawks and early peregine falcons are over the marsh. One marsh hawk was seen catching an immature clapper rail on September 8, 1983. The young rail was retrieved and examined. It had completed its molt. It had some growing to do as it weighed only 6 ounces, compared to the 10–16 ounces of an adult. Most of the southbound peregrines follow the coast line flying along over the beach, feeding to some extent on shorebirds. I have not seen any pursue a clapper rail.

9.

FALL MIGRATION AND
THE HUNTING SEASON

Migration

Most information on fall migration is based on recoveries of banded birds taken by hunters, and on concentrations of birds noted along the southward migration route where they had not previously been seen in such numbers.

From banding studies, it is apparent that late August and Setpember is the time that most clapper rails from the Middle Atlantic states begin their departure for the wintering grounds. In trapping at Chincoteague, Stewart (1951b) noted on August 25, 1951, that there was an increase in fully grown young rails in traps. He suggests that this indicates that the first major migration movement was underway at the time. Banding at Tuckerton, New Jersey, indicates that many rails had left that area about a week or 10 days before September 1, just before the hunting season opens (Mangold, 1974). Evidence that some birds migrate early is known by the record of one banded at Chincoteague, August 15, 1950, and recovered about 60 miles to the south on September 6, 1950.

At Cape May, New Jersey, Witmer Stone (1937) states that his earliest date indicating southward migration was August 28, 1922, "when several were found near South Cape May where none had been seen before and others on dry ground just behind the sand dunes, evidently birds that had dropped down from their night flight."

The route taken by clapper rails as they leave Chincoteague is shown by 13 of Stewart's banded birds that were recovered in Virginia at distances of 10 to 60 miles farther south. These recoveries were made in Accomack and Northampton counties. Seven were taken in the vicinity of Mockhorn Island, about 50 miles south of the banding station. The Mockhorn Island area, located near the southern tip of the Eastern Shore of Virginia, may be an important concentration point for migrating and wintering clapper rails; but it is also a state public shooting area. Ornithologist Harry Armistead found a dead clapper rail at the top of the 191-foot lighthouse at Smith Island, which is located next to Mockhorn (letter of June 18, 1981). At Cape Charles, the southern tip of the Eastern Shore Peninsula, clapper rails take off across the 19-mile stretch of open water at the mouth of Chesapeake Bay, heading toward Back Bay (south of Norfolk) and the North Carolina border.

Although most of the Back Bay marshes are fresh, the rails apparently follow a route that takes them through that area, which is located close to the coast. Some may fly over and some are known to stop. During the fall migration of 1956, Federal Game Agent Robert Halstead told Biologists David Adams and Tom Quay (1958) that on October 1, game agents picked up 50–75 dead clapper rails beneath telephone wires in the Back Bay area. Three days later in marshes near Southport in southeastern North Carolina, Agent Halstead observed a heavy concentration of clapper rails, 25–30 at a time during high tide. They were quite vociferous and seemed to be at a temporary stopover during their migration. The next day, October 5, Adams was in the same area, and although clapper rails seemed plentiful, such concentrations as those that Halstead reported were not present. Thus, the birds apparently moved on in one day.

While some local breeding birds from New Jersey and Virginia arrive along the southeastern coast in September, most arrive in October and November. Most local clapper rail populations from Long Island, New Jersey, and Virginia winter in the South Atlantic area, from about North Carolina to northeastern Florida, with greatest numbers in South Carolina and Georgia (see Table 8 and Fig. 36).

Some rails waste little time in traveling from their breeding grounds to the wintering area. This is indicated by an immature bird that was banded at Chincoteague on August 26, 1950, and recovered in northeastern Florida on September 24, 1950; and a bird banded at Chincoteague August 7, 1951, was recovered along

Table 8. Clapper Rail Recoveries along the Atlantic Coast*

Where Banded	Where Recovered	Number
New York	South Carolina	1
	Georgia	2
	Florida	1
New Jersey	Virginia	8
	North Carolina	4
	South Carolina	30
	Georgia	38
	Florida	4
Maryland	Virginia	1
Virginia	North Carolina	5
	South Carolina	14
	Georgia	8
	Florida	6
North Carolina	South Carolina	2
	Georgia	2
Georgia	Florida	1

the Georgia coast in September of the same year. One of two New Jersey clapper rails banded during the breeding season was recaptured in South Carolina on September 14, the other in Georgia on September 17.

A few Chincoteague clapper rails banded in late summer were still there in October (17 recoveries) and November (4); and several clappers banded during the breeding season in New Jersey were recovered in Virginia in October and November. Since most of the recoveries in the fall are by hunters, and most of the hunting is in September and October, until further means of recapture are attempted, the status of local birds wintering remains to be determined.

In some years, sizable numbers of clapper rails are reported on the annual Christmas Counts in late December at Chincoteague

*Clapper rails banded during the breeding season and late summer and recovered in the fall south of state where banded.

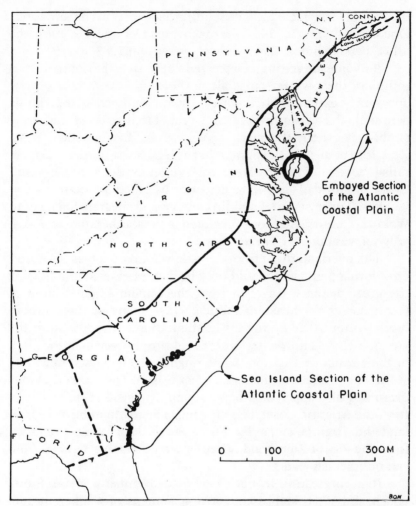

Fig. 36. Recoveries in South Atlantic states of clapper rails banded by R. E. Stewart on the Eastern Shore of Virginia. Banding locations are included within large open circle, while recoveries are represented by dots. Illustration courtesy of R. E. Stewart.

and Cape Charles along the Virginia coast. Some of these may be local birds, or birds from New York or New Jersey. There was recovery of a bird banded along the Virginia coast on September 1, 1971, and recaptured in the same general area in January 1973. This may have been a local bird or it may have come from farther north. There are two direct recoveries of New Jersey clapper rails indicating that at least a few local breeding birds winter in the same area. One banded May 25, 1967, was recovered December 5, 1967; the other, banded June 1, 1969, was recovered January 26, 1970.

As some migrating clapper rails approach the southern terminus of their winter range along the southeastern coast, a few apparently extend their flight southwestward across the Florida peninsula to the northwest Gulf Coast of that state; or some may simply overshoot the mark or wander in that direction. R. C. Crawford et al. (1983) reported that at least a few northern clapper rails (*Rallus longirostris crepitans*) winter on the northwest Gulf Coast of Florida. They have evidence based on 3 specimens collected at Turkey Point, Franklin County, and one from Shell Point, Wakulla County. Also, one specimen of the southeastern race, *R. l. waynei* was taken at Turkey Point.

The overland flight from the Atlantic Coast across the northern Florida peninsula would only be a short extension following the great distance travelled from the Middle Atlantic coast to Georgia and northeastern Florida where many of the northern birds winter. Also, noting the configuration of the coast near the Georgia-Florida line, a few birds could simply overshoot the mark of their usual destination. Some might even be blown inland by storms or be offcourse for some other reason. There are numerous examples of clapper rails being found at considerable distances from the Atlantic Coast, i.e., the Appalachian Mountains of Maryland and Virginia, and at least four recorded appearances reported from the city of Richmond, Virginia, a considerable distance from salt or brackish water.

It is interesting to note that on November 4, 1966, Storrs Olsen and W.H. Hobbs collected specimens of 4 different subspecies of clapper rails (*crepitans, waynei, scotti,* and *saturatus*) in a single small area of salt marsh at Turkey Point (Crawford et al., 1983).

According to R. E. Stewart (1954), there was a recovery rate of 4.5 percent for clapper rails banded at Chincoteague. Of 46 banded rails that were later recovered, 45 were shot by hunters, and 1 was run over by a car. Forty-two were taken during the first hunting season within 4 months of date of banding; and 3 were taken between 12 and 16 months after banding, during the second hunting season. One immature bird banded on July 3, 1933, was shot during the fourth hunting season following banding, on October 29, 1936.

Hunting

September marks the opening of the clapper rail or marsh hen hunting season along most of the Atlantic Coast. Some say the first full moon in September signals the opening of the season. A full moon sometimes means that there will be an exceptionally high tide, known as a "marsh hen tide," which is necessary for successful hunting. Such a tide occurs when a north wind pushes the normal high tide up even higher, and along the Virginia coast, 2 or 3 feet above normal high tide may be sufficient for good shooting, whereas farther down the coast in South Carolina and Georgia, apparently higher tides are necessary. Under such conditions a boat can be poled through the marsh grass, flushing the birds (Fig. 37).

As indicated by John Oney (1954), who observed marsh hen hunting along the Georgia coast,

> It should be emphasized that the direction of the wind as it influences the height of the tide is an important factor in determining the number of hunters and their success. Frequently the conditions of the wind and tide appear to be correct for a successful hunt but the tide's rise, although high enough to permit travel in a boat over the marsh, is not high enough for a good kill. The resultant poor success is due to the birds reluctance to fly. Until a certain height of tide is reached the clapper rail will swim and dive at the approach of the hunter. As the tide becomes higher it can no longer escape in this manner and it will flush from the grass.

Warren Blandin, studying marsh hens in South Carolina (1965b), notes that one of the problems with marsh hen hunting is that you cannot always predict when there is going to be a marsh hen tide. "Tides are affected by the wind, as well as astronomical phenomena, thus many of the marsh hen tides are not predicted by tide tables, being the result of high northwest winds. Conversely, many predicted high tides do not occur because of southwesterly winds blowing offshore. . . . South Carolina rail hunters generally agree that a nine foot tide is necessary for good hunting. An 8.5 foot tide is considered a bare minimum." Table 9 shows the number of marsh hen tides occurring in Beaufort County, South Carolina, during Blandin's 5-year study.

Table 9. Number of Marsh Hen Tides in South Carolina, 1960–64*

Tide Height	1960	1961	1962	1963	1964
9.0 ft.	4	4	4	2	4
8.5 ft.	11	7	7	7	13

*from Blandin (1965b)

When there is a marsh hen tide, rails look for a high place in the marsh. Experienced hunters know this and head for duck blinds, where several of these birds may congregate.

The marsh hen is probably the easiest mark of any of the game birds, the reason being that the area in which they are hunted is wide open and the bird is a straight-ahead flier, often slowing down shortly after take-off to look for a place to descend and hide. But sometimes a marsh hen will take off for 100 yards or more, and once it gets underway may be flying as fast as a black duck.

Fig. 37. Hunting marsh hens in the salt marsh. It is necessary to have an above-normal high tide (a spring tide) in order to pole a boat through the marsh and flush the birds. Illustration: John W. Taylor.

By September 1, a few young marsh hens from late hatches are still unable or barely able to fly. In New Jersey in 1950, Schmidt and McLain (1951) reported that 177 hunters they contacted killed 1,226 marsh hens; 206 of these were not able to fly as their flight feathers were not fully developed. And, in a series of 80 birds taken in late September 1983 in Accomack County, Virginia, 6 birds had their new flight feathers only half unsheathed.

A few hunters stalk marsh hens at low tide with an approach known as "muddin'." At low tide marsh hens sometimes come out on the flats to feed and are an easy target. However, not many birds are killed by this method as the going is slow and there is a lot of waiting for a single bird to occasionally expose itself to the gunner.

The usual method of hunting marsh hens in Louisiana coastal marshes, where the tides are lower, is reported by Hugh Bateman in *Louisiana Conservationist* (1965):

> Most rail hunting is done in the early morning and late evening hours and preferably during high tide since they are most active and apt to flush at these times. The most popular method of hunting rails in Louisiana employs the use of several people, several dogs, if available, and as much noise as possible. As many as four to six persons fan out abreast 30–40 yards apart. Several dogs of the retriever (not pointing) strain are then positioned to roam back and forth within gun range ahead of this line of hunters. The whole group then begins to sweep across the marsh hollering and making as much noise as possible. This may sound a little ridiculous but rails are characteristically weak fliers and are usually very reluctant to do so. All the encouragement possible is needed to make them rise clumsily to wing out of the thick marsh grass. Once the victim is airborne, the shooting is easy as the rail offers no fancy aerial antics but lumbers off slowly in a straight line away from the hunters.
>
> Since the shots had are usually at close range, an open bore 16 or 20 gauge gun is preferred using 7½ or 8 shot in light field loads.

According to Robert Mangold (writing in *Management of Migratory Shore and Upland Game Birds in North America,* 1977), few states have quantitative data on clapper rail harvests:

> In recent years, estimates for New Jersey indicate about 3,000 hunters with a seasonal bag of about 15,000 clapper rails. In 1947, the last year in which hunters were allowed to use motors, about 85,000 clappers were harvested in Georgia; in 1948 and 1956, the harvests were about

25,000 and 52,000 respectively. In 1972, about 4,000 hunters bagged from 50,000 to 75,000 clappers. In South Carolina, a 1966 estimate indicated that 5,775 hunters harvested nearly 74,000 clapper rails; in recent years, the total bag has been estimated as probably less than 14,000. North Carolina estimates the lack of huntable territory has reduced the current harvest to less than 500.

In the early 1980s, daily bag limits were usually 10 birds in the Northeastern states, and 15 along the South Atlantic Coast. The length of the hunting season is from early September into November in most Atlantic Coast states, except South Carolina, where it runs from early October to mid-December.

A few king rails are killed by clapper rail hunters in coastal salt marshes. Hunters Gordon Clark and Tom Reed killed 3 kings and 50 clappers in 2 days of hunting at Chincoteague, Virginia, during September 1961 (personal communication, Clark).

Some hunters along the Eastern Shore of Virginia cut off the head, wings, and legs, and skin the rail as they would skin a muskrat, turning the hide or skin inside out.

10.

THE CLAPPER RAIL IN WINTER

During the winter, clapper rails occur along the Atlantic Coast from southern New England southward. Comparatively few spend the winter in the northern part of the range, i.e., southeastern Connecticut and the New York City-Long Island section. On the basis of band recoveries and Christmas Counts, it is apparent that the greatest wintering concentrations are in the South Atlantic area, mostly in coastal South Carolina, Georgia, and northeastern Florida. In milder winters, sizable numbers occur along the Virginia and North Carolina coasts.

Information on winter populations is compiled mainly from the National Audubon Society Christmas Counts. Such counts are made at many points along the coast during one day each winter, usually between December 18 and January 2. The count area, usually in the same place year after year, is a circle 15 miles in diameter. Each participant has an assigned territory within the circle. As many as 50 persons or more may take part in some of the coastal counts. The number of species and the number of individuals of each species are tallied. One of the objectives of Christmas Counts is to note trends in winter populations.

The number of clapper rails reported on Christmas Counts varies greatly from year to year in some localities, due probably to actual changes in populations, but also due to weather conditions and variation in the number of participants. Harry Armistead (letter of June 18, 1981), coordinator of the Cape Charles, Virginia, Christmas Count, informed me that all of the *Spartina alterniflora* marsh areas have clappers in the count areas, but of course depending on tide, wind, amount of ice, or cold weather prior to the count, their abundance varies greatly, as does their detectability, especially if it is very windy. Some cold years we only get a few. In the right weather veritable choruses sound off. Virtually all counts are based on calls, as very few rails are seen in the winter marsh.

There are doubtless more birds in the marshes than reported in the Christmas Counts. For example, only 6 clapper rails were reported on the 1983 Chincoteague Christmas Count. Fred Scott (personal communication), coordinator of the count, felt that the low count was probably due to the intense cold spell of December 24–25, which may have caused some birds to shift southward. There are approximately 18,000 acres of salt marsh in the Chincoteague Christmas Count circle.

Approximately one month after the count, on January 29, 1984, I spent a day in a 50-acre marsh section of the circle along the Chincoteague causeway, and found evidence of 8 clappers. I saw 2 along 2 tidal guts and found fresh evidence of 6 others along 6 other guts. Since the guts were separated by at least 200 feet, and my observations were made in a period of approximately 2 hours, moving in one direction, it is unlikely that a bird would have moved between 2 such widely separated guts. During the Christmas Count no birds were reported from the causeway, where participants gather most of their evidence from calling rails.

It is not too likely that clapper rails would shift southward during the winter and return a month later unless there was a solid

Table 10. Numbers of Clapper Rails Reported on Some Christmas Counts*

Location	Year	Count
New York City area (Nassau, Queens, and Brooklyn, combined)	1951	55
New Jersey (state total)	1972	107
Crisfield, Maryland	1975	23
Chincoteague, Virginia	1975	159
Cape Charles, Virginia	1971	155
Morehead City, North Carolina	1982	21
Hilton Head, South Carolina	1975	61
Glynn County, Georgia	1982	105
Sapelo Island, Georgia	1974	117
Jacksonville, Florida	1975	920
St. Augustine, Florida	1975	323

*From *Audubon Field Notes* and *American Birds.*

freeze, which seldom occurs in coastal tidewater areas at this latitude. I would therefore recommend that in the Middle Atlantic states, during Christmas Counts, greater effort might be made to census rails by track counts (Fig. 38) along tidal guts, a method that might not be practical in the South Atlantic coastal area where many more clappers winter.

The high counts in most years at Cape Charles, Virginia, are probably due to a funneling of migrants into the narrow tip of the Eastern Shore peninsula, and the facing of the wide mouth of Chesapeake Bay beyond. An added factor is the high number of

Fig. 38. Rail tracks at low tide.

persons participating in the counts there. Chincoteague, 70 miles
north of Cape Charles, also has high concentrations of rails in
some years from this same "narrowing" effect of the peninsula and
the extensive optimum habitat. Christmas Counts at Cape
Charles and Chincoteague in the 13-year period 1970–82 *(Audubon Field Notes* and *American Birds)* are as follows:

Cape Charles		Chincoteague	
1970	39	1970	14
1971	155	1971	13
1972	99	1972	26
1973	127	1973	25
1974	146	1974	84
1975	141	1975	159
1976	37	1976	51
1977	13	1977	10
1978	44	1978	29
1979	149	1979	29
1980	13	1980	6
1981	20	1981	5
1982	26	1982	4

Christmas Counts at Jacksonville and St. Augustine also are
usually higher than at other areas along the coast, apparently
because the resident population is augmented by migrants from
the north reaching the southern terminus of their range:

Jacksonville		St. Augustine	
1974	765	1974	108
1975	920	1975	323
1976	742	1976	683
1977	380	1977	443
1978	633	1978	214
1979	273	1979	210
1980	138	1980	161
1981	127	1981	28
1982	471	1982	84

The clapper rail also winters in many estuaries away from the
coast. In the Chesapeake Bay country, they occur as far north as
Annapolis; along the James River, at least to Hog Island opposite
Jamestown; and up the Rappahannock to Tappahannock. Across

the river from Tappahannock, I have encountered muskrat trap-
pers in brackish marshes that have inadvertently caught both
clapper and king rails. Rails use muskrat trails or leads in passage
through such brackish marshes.

There is little published information on the behavior of clapper rails on the wintering grounds. I have made some observations
on clapper rails at Chincoteague at that season. Two birds that I
observed on January 29 and 30, 1984, had territories along stretches
of about 50 feet of their respective tidal guts and adjacent tall-grass
Spartina alterniflora. On both days, temperatures were in the 30s
in the morning and low 40s (F°) in the midafternoon; and at 8:00
A.M., the short-grass zone away from the guts was frozen, but the
tall-grass zone, where there was tidal action along the gut, was
unfrozen.

It was possible to determine the extent of what might have
been temporary territories along the gut and adjacent narrow tall-
grass zone by the fresh tracks, many fresh droppings, and fresh
regurgitated pellets. The tidal guts averaged 3 to 4 feet in width,
and at low tide, with 2 or 3 inches of water in the gut, it was
possible to see the many trails made by the single line of tracks
back and forth along the twisting gut. A bird would leave the gut
from time to time, walk over to the adjacent mud bank, and probe
for common or square-backed fiddler crabs. Along the edge of one
gut I counted 35 droppings and 40 regurgitated pellets, indicating
that the bird had been using that section of the gut for some time.
When later examined the pellets mostly contained fragments of
fiddler crabs.

Roth et al. (1972) found in their radio telemetry study in
Louisiana marshes that clapper rails had an average minimum
home range of 533 yards in winter, with an average daily movement of 155 yards.

Additional information on winter behavior was noted in the
early 1960s as I watched the behavior of captive clapper and king
rails in a cage that I had at a pond at the Patuxent Wildlife Research
Center. During extended freezes or when there was snow on the
ground and the pond was frozen, water for drinking was obtained
by ingesting snow or small chunks of ice.

Captive clapper and king rails preferred to rest on the ice
rather than in a more protected section of the cage that was pro-
vided with a windbreak and a bedding of straw. During alternate

periods of freezing and thawing, spherical chunks of ice, up to the size of a baseball, stuck to the tails of the clapper rails, and smaller particles stuck to their breasts. Strangely, particles of ice virtually never adhered to the plumage of the king rails.

In the wild during freezing weather, clapper rails in some sections may be hard put to survive, as illustrated by an encounter witnessed by Guy Willey (1977) in the marshlands of the Blackwater River in southern Dorchester County, Maryland.

For 2 weeks in mid-January 1977, minimum temperatures at Cambridge ranged between 1° and 20° F., with maximum temperatures continuously below 40°. The result was an almost complete freeze of the Blackwater River. Willey's account continues:

> On January 23, my sons . . . made a late afternoon visit with me to my property on Shorters Warf [sic] Road near Blackwater National Wildlife Refuge. There was a small area of open water, about 2 by 6 feet, at each end of a culvert, where a Great Blue Heron *(Ardea herodias)* and a clapper rail *(Rallus longirostris)* had been feeding since about the first of January. When we arrived this time the Great Blue Heron was standing in the open water and had caught a rail that we believed to be the same one we had been seeing there. The heron flew off to a cleared area with its prey. We made no effort to run the heron away from the rail, which appeared near death. For two minutes we watched the heron devour the rail, and then we left.

11.

NATURAL CATASTROPHES, PREDATION, AND POLLUTION

Natural Catastrophes

Floods, fogs, coastal storms, and hurricanes often have a devastating effect, for the short term, on clapper rail populations. Such effects are usually local, however, and time after time clapper rails have demonstrated a remarkable resilience following a catastrophe. Alex Sprunt and Burnham Chamberlain in their book *South Carolina Birdlife* (1949) have pointed this out: "Illustrative of the species' ability to survive natural catastrophes is the fact that, though A. H. DuPre and W. P. Baldwin, of the U.S. Fish and Wildlife Service estimated that fifteen thousand were killed on the South Carolina coast by the hurricane of August 11, 1940, they soon returned to their normal numbers." And in New Jersey in August 1976, Shoemaker and Widjeskog (1973–77) reported that Hurricane Belle caused the deaths of an estimated 20,000 young and adult clapper rails, based on surveys of the storm drift line. The population apparently recovered within the next several years.

    Fog. In migrating southward clapper rails may sometimes be blown inland by storms or confused by fogs. In a paper by Adams and Quay (1958), John H. Farrell reported that at dusk on September 20, 1955, hundreds of clapper rails invaded Carolina Beach, North Carolina, preceding and during a heavy fog. "The birds became confused and entered shops, flew into cars and people, perched on telephone wires and houses, etc." (I cannot think of anything more unrail-like than a clapper rail perched on a telephone wire!) Also apprently due to fog, numbers of clapper rails migrating northward in April 1982 were reported by Tom Gwynn (personal communication) to be on the Chesapeake Bay Bridge that crosses the mouth of Chesapeake Bay between Norfolk and Cape Charles, Virginia.

Flood Tides. Excessively high tides that occur during the nesting season can have a devastating effect on clapper rail populations (Fig. 39). Rails build their nests high enough so that their eggs are several inches above the normal high tide mark. Sometimes a flood tide reaches the level of the eggs, or may rise slightly above, covering them. Several authors have suggested that when this happens, the tide only remains at that level for a short period, and when it recedes the eggs often are not damaged, and will eventually hatch. These authors have failed to point out that some eggs may be well incubated and, when the water rises to their level, would float away, unless the incubating bird can remain on the nest. As Ivan Tomkins (1958) points out (referring to hobby egg-collecting in the early 1900s): "It used to be customary for egg collectors to carry a small can of fresh water and test all eggs found. If the eggs floated, incubation was too far advanced to blow the eggs through a small hole in one side."

Fig. 39. Dead marsh grass left on wharf as flood tide receded along Gargathy Creek near Metomkin Island, Virginia. Clapper rails are common nesting birds in the salt marsh across the creek. If the flood tide had occurred a month later, at the height of the nesting season in late May, virtually all nests would have been destroyed.

If water does not rise too far above normal high tide, nests are usually built up by the rails as the tide slowly rises; thus, the eggs may not be destroyed as the birds are still able to continue to cover them (Meanley, 1967; Jackson, 1983).

Destruction of eggs is eventually compensated for by the large clutches the species lays (9–14 eggs), by renesting, and by some clappers raising 2 clutches in one season. But if the flood tide is accompanied by high winds and wave action, the nesting season may be a disaster. In the nesting season of 1982, at Chincoteague, ornithologist John Buckalew (1982) estimated nest losses at 80 percent due to above-normal high tides. And at Beaufort County, South Carolina, Blandin reported a 50 percent nest loss due to flooding in one of his study areas in 1964.

Flooding can also be devastating to young clapper rail broods, as witnessed by O. S. Pettingill, Jr. (1938), at Cobb Island, Virginia. Dr. Pettingill recounts his observations of a clapper rail brood during a flood tide along this Atlantic Coast section of the Eastern Shore of Virginia, July 3, 1933:

> During the high tide I stayed in Captain George W. Cobb's House. This was ideally located on the southern end of the island and afforded an extensive view of a large portion of the islands to the north. Placed back from the beach behind a ridge of sand dunes, the house rested on piles some seven or eight feet above the salt marsh that began below the house and stretched far to the northwestward and westward. Protected thus from high water and the surf, it was a safe place under such conditions.
>
> The tide that occurred on this day completely inundated the marsh and came to within one foot of the floor of Captain Cobb's house. While this tide was rising, I counted six pairs of adult Clapper Rails and their broods swimming above the marsh, striving desperately to reach the dunes, which were the only parts of the island still above water. But the northeast wind was driving them to the southward and made their attempts at reaching shore seemingly useless. Two broods ultimately came ashore; three others were swept past the southern point of the island to death in the rough ocean. The sixth brood was blown directly toward the house. My attention was naturally directed toward the welfare of the family group.
>
> As this brood rapidly drifted toward the house, I was able to discern seven young birds, all of which were about of an equal age. I judged that they were two weeks old. They were barely able to keep their heads and backs above water. Waves, freshly whipped up by the

wind, continually washed over them, soaking their down and making them less buoyant each time. They seemed about to succumb and were making no attempts to swim. The two parent birds, however, were large enough and strong enough to keep their heads above the waves breaking over them and were swimming anxiously about their young. Every now and then the old birds would head toward the dunes but, seeing that their offspring were not following, would turn back and continue circling them. In a very short time the rail family was floating along past the house. Captain Cobb and I soon rescued the seven young birds by plunging into the water gathering them up and bringing them to the porch. We placed them in a carton two feet square and closed the four flaps. As a result of our interference the parent birds made away to the sand dunes calling loudly. Darkness set in before the tide went out, and the young rails passed the night in the carton on the porch. While their down was soaked and they seemed utterly exhausted, scarcely moving when we touched them, they were old enough and the temperature of the surrounding air was warm enough to permit their survival without brooding.

At sunrise the next morning we were awakened by the calling of the young birds in the carton and the noisy clatter of the parent birds which were frantically searching about beneath the house. Looking through the window on to the porch, we saw one parent bird fly to the porch floor and walk directly to the carton. Several times it walked around the box, striking at the sides as it did so. It jumped nimbly to the top and picked up the loose end of the flaps with its bill, lifted it up, and flipped it over backward. This allowed a small opening between the two underlying flaps, through which it thrust its head. Immediately, it made a quick thrust at one of the young birds. To us it appeared as if the old bird had actually grasped one of the young birds, but the young bird was too large to be drawn through the opening. Consequently the adult let go and remained on the box, continuing its clatter. When we went out on the porch to open the box, the old bird flew to the marsh grass below. The young birds were strong enough to hop out hurriedly, jump down from the porch and follow their parent away. We last saw the young birds going through the marsh grass, responding to the coaxing sounds of the parent.

Sometimes during an above-normal high tide or flood tide, a clapper rail will carry a downy chick in its bill to safety. E. Burnham Chamberlain of the Charleston, South Carolina, museum told Ivan Tomkins (1937) of seeing an adult clapper rail carrying its young:

It seems that he, with several others, was at Procher's [Porcher's] Bluff, South Carolina, during a time of high tide. As they were watching young rails drifting by on the usual drift trash, he noticed an adult rail swimming with something in its bill. Through binoculars he could see that the bird was carrying a young chick in such a manner that its head was under water. As he watched she stopped, shifted the burden so the young would not drown, swam to the raft of drift, dumped the chick on to it, and clambered up herself.

Hurricanes.   An interesting account of clapper and king rail behavior in the storm tides of a hurricane in the Louisiana coastal marsh country was reported by Robert J. Newman from information based on eyewitness accounts of H. W. Belknap, a graduate student from Louisiana State University, and J. H. Sutherlin, Manager of Sabine National Wildlife Refuge. Hurricane Audrey was Louisiana's worst coastal storm of the present century and struck with its greatest force along the southwest Louisiana coast on the morning of June 27, 1957. Newman's report was as follows:

> Rafts of marsh debris, ranging in size from 10 × 10 to 20 × 100 feet went floating by (HWB,JSS). On them huddled a strange company of water moccasins, nutria, rails, and gallinules—sometimes as many as 20 birds to a raft. Occasionally as the great rollers surged forward, the mats of vegetation would buckle and disintegrate. Then, according to Sutherlin, the Purple Gallinules would drown, but the suposely less aquatic Clapper or King Rails would swim adeptly away through the rough water and flying spindrift.
>
> The rain-drenched lawn at Sabine headquarters became a sanctuary within a sanctuary. The wildlife congregated there included water snakes, a marsh deer, a skunk, armadillos, and 200 to 250 King or Clapper Rails.

Winter Freeze of 1976–1977.   Fred Ferrigno of the New Jersey Division of Fish, Game and Wildlife, indicated to me that the servere winter freeze of 1976–77 along the Atlantic Coast, which extended into the South Atlantic wintering range of the clapper rail, had a devastating effect on northeastern breeding populations. Nesting success in 3 New Jersey study areas combined was down by approximately two-thirds in the spring of 1977 from that of the spring of 1976 (letter to the author, July 31, 1984).

Predation

Raccoons.   Raccoons are well-known plunderers of bird nests both in dryland and wetland habitats. Some coastal barrier island salt marshes are isolated from raccoons, but most studies of clapper rails in coastal salt marshes reported nests damaged by them. The extent of depredations by that mammal in most clapper rail nesting areas is unknown, but the abundance of breeding rail populations in many coastal marshes would indicate that the raccoon is not a serious limiting factor in nesting success of the overall population.

However, along the Alabama coast, Holliman (1981) reported that the raccoon was the principal predator of clapper rail nests in his study area. He noted 28 nests destroyed by raccoons. In South Carolina, Blandin (1965b) reported that the raccoon was a major cause of nest predation, causing 73.8 percent of all predatory nest losses (48 of 65 nests). It should be pointed out that paths made to nests by persons conducting rail nest studies make it easier for raccoons to find those nests.

At Taylor's Gut, Delaware, where fingers of the marsh extend inland toward the mainland, 'coons were always present in my study areas. They would enter the tidal gut at low tide and dig for Baltic clams (*Macoma*) at the same spot where clapper and king rails were seen to do the same.

The Fish Crow.   Fish crows are usually thought of as the chief plunderer of clapper rail eggs (Fig. 40). The extent of their depredations appears to depend on the amount of shrub and tree cover near the marsh and the number of other birds, particularly shorebirds, seabirds, herons, and egrets nesting near a salt marsh, that act to some extent as a buffer.

In the wide open marsh area along the Chincoteague causeway where there are few shrubs and virtually no trees, I seldom see more than a half-dozen fish crows during a given day, except in the evening when others fly across the marsh to their roosts. There is a high nesting density of rails and laughing gulls in the area. The crows seem to take mostly gull eggs, which are completely exposed during the laying period in their open nests, in contrast to the eggs of the clapper rail which are partially concealed by a canopy over the nest. Because of the few eggshells noted at crow feeding stations near the causeway, it would seem that depredations on rail and gull nests in the area is very light.

Fig. 40. Fish crow hunting for clapper rail nests. Illustration: John W. Taylor.

In his South Carolina study area in 1963, Blandin (1965b) reported that some 24 of 56 nests were destroyed by fish crows; and at Wakulla Beach, Florida, William G. Fargo (1927) reported that at a fish crow feeding station under a small pine he found the remains of 79 or more clapper rail eggs, one willet egg, two Wilson's plover eggs, several turtle eggs, one fish head, and one rock crab.

The Marsh Hawk. The marsh hawk or harrier is a known predator of clapper rails. The extent of its predation on clappers, however, is not well known, as there is little documented evidence based on stomach or pellet examinations of this raptor.

Several South Carolina authors have reported that the marsh hawk is an important predator of the clapper rail in that state. However, none to my knowledge have presented pertinent evidence of such importance. Apparently their statements are based on their (or someone else's) witnessing marsh hawks catching or feeding on clappers.

According to Arthur T. Wayne (1910), "The Marsh Hawk is an exceedingly abundant winter resident on and near the coast. . . . This species destroys numbers of Wayne's Clapper Rails *(Rallus crepitans waynei)*, which it catches with ease." Wayne further states that "I have often heard it shriek when the Marsh Hawk *(Circus hudsonius)* was attacking it." Wayne's home was next to a salt marsh so he was well located to observe the marsh hawk in action.

In the sizable series of stomach analysis cards in the files of the U.S. Fish and Wildlife Service, most of the material is from interior locations, away from the salt marsh. The remains of a clapper rail were found in a marsh hawk stomach from Wallop's Island, near Chincoteague, and in a marsh hawk stomach from St. Helena Island, South Carolina. R. E. Stewart (1951a) found 2 freshly killed clapper rails at Chincoteague in an area where he observed a hunting marsh hawk; and as stated above, on September 8, 1983, at Chincoteague, I saw a marsh hawk capture an immature clapper rail, which I retrieved (Fig. 41).

Dr. Van T. Harris (1952) of the U.S. Fish and Wildlife Service examined 79 pellets from the Blackwater River salt and brackish marsh in Dorchester County, Maryland, that he believed were those of marsh hawks. The analysis indicated that 73.4 percent of the pellets contained remains of meadow voles *(Microtus pennsylvanicus)*, 15.2 percent rice rats, and 3.8 percent unidentified small mammals; the remaining percentage was not reported. Clapper rails occur in this marsh, but not in the numbers found in salt marshes closer to the Atlantic Coast.

Short-eared Owl. R. F. Johnston (1956) reported that clapper rail remains were identified in three samples of short-eared owl pellets from along the California coast. Although fairly common in Atlantic Coast marshes in winter, it feeds mainly on prey smaller than the clapper rail.

Laughing and Herring Gulls. There are a few reported examples of laughing gulls preying on downy young clapper rails (see Chapter 7). I have found the remains of clapper rail chicks in herring gull nesting colonies at Chincoteague. It was not known if the chicks were taken alive or as carrion. Where laughing gulls and

Fig. 41. Marsh hawk or northern harrier with prey. The extent of marsh hawk depredations on clapper rails is not well known. Illustration: John W. Taylor.

clapper rails nest close together in the same marshes, there is a potential for some predation of the former on the latter's downy young; but gulls are not a significant threat to the overall rail population, as the clapper is much more widely distributed. In the Chincoteague area, Marshall Howe (1982) cites an incident of predation by a laughing gull on a willet chick.

Pollution

The Georgia Department of Natural Resources has been monitoring mercury levels in wildlife in the coastal region since 1971, when high levels of mercury were found in clapper rails in the Turtle River near Brunswick. Highest concentrations were found in birds living in marshes close to an industrial plant. Mercury levels exceeded the .5 ppm limit, as set by the U.S. Food and Drug Administration, in 93.5 percent of all clapper rail muscle samples. Mercury contamination continued to be a problem in the Bruns-

wick area through the 1970s, although the effect on local clapper
rail populations is unknown, and the population is still numerous.
But comparable levels found in other species of birds from similarly contaminated areas have in some cases been lethal. During
the period of the investigation, the Georgia Game and Fish Division stated that clapper rails from the Turtle River section near
Brunswick should not be eaten (R. Odum, 1980).

DDT and Mosquito Control.   The spraying of DDT for control of salt marsh mosquitoes in the 1960s along the Middle Atlantic coast led to high levels of residues of the compound in soils
of some salt marshes. DDT residues in the soil were of such a
magnitude that clapper rails scarcely could avoid prolonged expo-
sure to the compound. However, there was no evidence of die-offs
from such operations.

In 1967 and 1968, A. Van Velzen and J. F. Kreitzer (1975) of the
Patuxent Wildlife Research Center conducted experiments with
captive clapper rails to determine the toxicity of DDT to that
species. The authors concluded that "high resistence of the Clapper Rail to DDT indicates that the presence of that compound in
marshes is not likely to be a significant factor in mortality of adult
rails." And clapper rails are more resistant to that compound than
are a number of other birds inhabiting salt marshes. However,
long-term effects on reproduction have not been evaluated.

In New Jersey, mosquito control today is largely concentrated
in the salt hay *(Spartina patens)* marshes rather than the saltmarsh
cordgrass *(S. alterniflora)* marshes where most of the clapper rails
occur (Widjeskog and Shoemaker, 1983).

Foraging Effect of Greater Snow Geese on Rail Nesting Habitat

Widjeskog and Shoemaker (1983) reported a considerable reduc-
tion in clapper rail nesting cover in Atlantic County, New Jersey,
in the past 20 years, due to the foraging of greater snow geese.

12.

POSTSCRIPT

The clapper rail, a secretive bird, occasionally exposes itself in some extraordinary way.

George Reiger, in his book *Wanderer On My Native Shore* (1983), recounts the time he was waiting in a duck blind for some action, and he and a clapper rail played peekaboo, "with the bird peering at me from the roof in a curious upside-down fashion and me trying to sneak my hand up to grab the bird's downcurved bill before it could pull away. The game went on for half an hour, and I never did catch the rail—or shoot a duck." There was probably an extremely high tide at the time of this episode. Under these conditions, clappers often seek such an "island" in the marsh.

In *The Bird Life of Texas*, by H. C. Oberholser (1974), the following is noted: "In localities where it is not molested, the Clappers can become quite tame. Connie Hagar likes to relate that in the days prior to World War II—before progress changed everything—one or two Clapper Rails would often stride in from nearby marshes to stroll about inside the U. S. Post Office at Rockport, Texas." I wonder if this also was during high water?

Witmer Stone, writing in *Bird Studies at Old Cape May* (1937), states that "once in early Autumn when standing on the Meadows a Mud Hen alarmed at something came running rapidly through the grass and crouched suddenly directly between my feet doubtless thinking that he had found safety between two convenient lumps of mud and I did not abuse his confidence."

I was involved in a somewhat similar episode with the tiny black rail that we were trying to obtain for the specimen collection of the U.S. Fish and Wildlife Service. In June 1958, at Elliott Island, Maryland, at about midnight, Bob Stewart, John Webb, and I tried a technique where the three of us walked about the marsh as we stalked a calling bird; the man in the middle had a shotgun, and the one on each side held a flashlight. When a rail began calling from a position of 20 or 30 feet in front of us, the men holding the flashlight crossed the beams or triangulated on the spot from which the calling appeared to come. Then the man in the center would shoot at the spot where the beams crossed. But a minute or so after each shot, the bird would start calling from the side or behind us. After a half-dozen unsuccessful attempts at shooting the bird, I attempted to stalk it and capture it by hand. Each time the bird called, I approached the spot and often came within 3 or 4 feet, whereupon it would stop calling and move a few yards away. Finally, after a period of about 5 minutes of silence, it began calling again, close to me, and as I pointed my flashlight downward in the short marsh grass, I could see it standing right between my feet. It was an exciting moment as I reached down and grabbed the little black rail. It was kept alive in captivity for 2 years and was made into a specimen only after it had died.

Appendix 1.

THE SUBSPECIES OR GEOGRAPHIC RACES OF CLAPPER RAILS OF THE UNITED STATES

The subspecies, geographic races, or varieties of clapper rails have been described mainly on characteristics of plumage and size, and each is associated with a separate geographic region during the breeding season. Only one subspecies in the United States, the northern clapper rail of the Northeast and the Middle Atlantic coasts, makes long migrations.

Northern clapper rail *(Rallus longirostris crepitans)*. Generally grayish color. In adult, back grayish, breast cinnamon buff, abdomen white, sides and flanks grayish barred with white, chin and upper throat white, cheeks neutral gray or bluish gray. Breeds from central New England coast to southeastern North Carolina. Winters in most of breeding range, but in greatest numbers along South Atlantic coast (South Carolina, Georgia, and northeastern Florida).

Wayne's clapper rail *(R. l. waynei)*. Resembles *crepitans*, but slightly smaller and darker, and underparts more ashy. Named for Arthur T. Wayne, South Carolina Low Country ornithologist of the late 1800s and early 1900s. Its breeding range is from southeastern North Carolina (Brunswick County) to the northeastern coast of Florida.

Mangrove clapper rail *(R. l. insularum)*. Similar to *waynei*, but smaller, and feathers of upperparts more broadly edged with grayish (Howell, 1932). Apparently restricted to Florida Keys.

Florida clapper rail *(R. l. scotti)*. Darkest upperparts of all geographic races of the species. Plumage similar to king rail, but darker and more olivaceous (less reddish); upperparts blackish brown shaded with grayish olive; breast cinnamon, shaded with olive brown (Howell). Named for W. E. D. Scott, naturalist and collector for museums who worked in Florida from the 1870s to the 1890s. Breeding range of this subspecies mainly on the west coast of Florida and east coast north to Jupiter. In south-central Florida on the Brighton Seminole Indian Reservation, Glades County, in January 1958, I saw two very dark rails that looked exactly like *scottii*. It is possible that birds of that race move across the lower part of the Florida peninsula since they are found on both coasts.

Louisiana clapper rail *(R. l. saturatus)*. A brownish clapper rail. Plumage closely resembles that of king rail, but with underparts less rufescent, duller. Difficult to distinguish between this race of the clapper and the king rail in the field. Both species may occur in same brackish marshes. Breeding range extends from extreme west coast of Florida to south Texas coast.

California clapper rail *(R. l. obsoletus)*. Plumage brownish, resembling king rail. Cheeks brownish rather than grayish like East Coast and Gulf Coast clappers. Breast light ochraceous-buff (light brown). Breeds in San Francisco area.

Light-footed rail *(R. l. levipes)*. Similar to *obsoletus*, but with darker back, and breast a richer tone of cinnamon. Occurs along the southern California coast.

Yuma clapper rail *(R. l. yumanensis)*. Plumage similar to *obsoletus* and *levipes*, except paler. Unusual in that it inhabits freshwater marshes along the Colorado River in southeastern California and southwestern Arizona.

More details of plumage are found in Oberholser (1937), and Ridgway and Friedmann (1941).

Appendix 2.

SEXING AND AGING CLAPPER RAILS

The sex and age composition of a game bird population tells us something about its well-being. The time and length of the hunting season, and bag limits depend upon such information.

Sexing

In species such as clapper rails, where the sexes have similar plumages and there is only a slight difference in size, specimens (dead birds) can be sexed internally by an examination of the gonads. Investigators have found that on the average, males weigh more than females; some larger females, however, may weigh as much as or more than smaller males (see Table 11).

In specimens of the geographic race *Rallus longirostris saturatus* (Louisiana clapper rail) from Grand Terre Island, Jefferson Parish, Louisiana, Hugh Bateman (1965) found that in a sample of 116 males and 158 females taken during the hunting season (October–November), the mean weight of males was 322 grams, with a range of 183 to 401 grams, that of females 257 grams, with a range of 174 to 319 grams. Bateman used a division point between the mean weight of each sex. He states that "by using 290 grams as a division point, the probability of misclassifying a clapper rail weighing more than 290 grams by calling it a male was about 2.9 per cent and a clapper rail that weighed less than 290 grams a female, 2.6 per cent. . . . The probability of misclassification using 290 grams as a division point for sexing clapper rails indicated a reasonably small per cent error, 5.5 per cent for all birds."

Bateman found that an analysis of variance based on weights (in grams) of 83 aged clapper rails indicated no significant difference between adult and juvenile (immature) clapper rails in Oc-

Table 11. Weights (in Grams) of Clapper and King Rails

CLAPPER RAIL

Accomack County, Virginia, September 1983 (Meanley)

Adult Male (14)		*Adult Female (6)*		*Immature Male (29)*		*Immature Female (31)*	
Range	Average	Range	Average	Range	Average	Range	Average
286.5–394.5	351.0	235.9–330.4	278.1	221.2–360.7	306.3	201.4–300.0	243.3

Beaufort County, South Carolina, October 1964 (Blandin, 1965a)*

Adult Male (17)		*Adult Female (33)*		*Immature Male (41)*		*Immature Female (23)*	
Range	Average	Range	Average	Range	Average	Range	Average
275–375	337	200–400	272	250–375	319	225–325	258

Jefferson Parish, Louisiana, October–November 1963–64 (Bateman, 1965)†

Adult Male (116)		*Adult Female (158)*	
Range	Average	Range	Average
183–401	332	174–319	257

KING RAIL

Stuttgart, Arkansas; Kent County, Delaware; Cameron Parish, Louisiana (Meanley, 1969)

Adult Male (9)		*Adult Female (9)*	
Range	Average	Range	Average
339.9–490.0	415.5	253.0–325.0	305.9

*Weights to nearest 25 grams; races: *R.l.c.* and/or *R.l.w.*
†Adults and immatures combined; race: *R.l.s.*

tober and November. It should be pointed out that most clapper rails nest earlier in Louisiana than along the Middle Atlantic coast, thus young of the year would probably be more mature in the fall when these determinations were made.

In most sets of standard museum measurements of clapper rails there is an overlap. Measurements of males average only slightly greater than females (Table 12). However, in New Jersey, Robert Mangold (1974) found (in a sample of 65 dead birds that were sexed internally) that sex of clapper rails could be determined externally by measuring certain extremities. "Three measurements were selected as particularly valuable; the longest toe length, as measured from the anterior side of the tarsus, when the foot is bent perpendicularly backwards, to the end of the nail; the length of the bill from the feather line; and the depth of the bill as measured at the distal end of the groove which runs from the nostril. It was found that when the bill length was 2½ inches or longer, the toe length 2½ inches or longer, and the bill depth was 18/64 inch depth or larger, the bird was invariably a male." These measurements are applicable to the northern clapper rails *(Rallus longirostris crepitans)*. However, in dealing with live birds, measurements are often difficult to make.

Aging

From late summer to at least early winter, the presence of a bursa in young birds of the year should distinguish them from adults. The Bursa of Fabricus is a glandular sac in the upper wall of the cloaca at its junction with the vent (Farner, 1960). The age of the bird can be determined by probing into and measuring the bursa (its stages of involution) during the bird's early life (Terres, 1980).

The color of the bill and the heel (bend in leg or joint between the tibiotarsus and tarsometatarsus) are fairly reliable aging criteria with live or freshly killed birds. In most adult birds the bill is an orange-yellow or orange-red from the base to at least the nares in the upper mandible, and usually slightly beyond in the lower. In the immature, at least in the early fall, color is less intense and usually a light yellow or straw color. The tongue and lining of the mouth in adults is orange-red, and yellowish in juveniles or immatures in early fall. The heel in adults is pinkish, but barely so in immatures; and the legs of some adults are a light yellow. An immature female collected at Chincoteague, September 8, 1983, had a faint orange color at the base of the bill and a yellowish-orange mouth lining. The eye (iris) of adults is reddish-orange. Immatures in early fall have dull brown irides or orange-brown irides.

Table 12. Measurements of Clapper and King Rails
(From Ridgway and Friedmann, 1941. All specimens were adults. All measurements are given in millimeters. Wing measurements are for the chord, from bend of wing to tip of longest primary.)

| | Clapper Rail *(R.l.c.)* | | | |
| | *Males** | | *Females†* | |
	Range	Average	Range	Average
Wing	142.5–159.5	151.1	135.5–160.0	146.8
Tail	55.0– 69.0	64.6	55.0– 69.5	61.9
Exposed culmen	55.0– 69.5	63.3	53.5– 67.0	59.6
Tarsus	48.0– 56.0	51.7	41.0– 56.0	48.1
Middle toe without claw	45.5– 53.5	48.8	40.0– 52.0	45.9

| | King Rail *(R.e.e.)* | | | |
| | *Males ‡* | | *Females §* | |
	Range	Average	Range	Average
Wing	159.0–177.0	163.4	147.0–162.0	154.3
Tail	56.0– 72.5	65.9	60.0– 70.0	64.4
Exposed culmen	58.0– 65.5	62.5	50.0– 63.0	61.9
Tarsus	52.0– 64.0	58.4	49.5– 58.0	54.0
Middle toe without claw	50.5– 60.5	55.1	46.0– 56.0	50.8

* 21 specimens from Mass., N.Y., N.J., Va., and N.C.
† 17 specimens from N.J., Va., and N.C.
‡ 18 specimens from Ill., Mo., D.C., Va., Ala., La., and S.C.
§ 14 specimens from Ill., D.C., Md., Va., La., and Fla.

Appendix 3.

METHODS OF CAPTURING RAILS
FOR BANDING

An assortment of devices have been employed in capturing clapper rails for banding purposes. The trap that I have found to be the most successful is known as the all-purpose or cloverleaf trap. This trap was designed by Seth H. Low for capturing shorebirds. Using this device, Robert E. Stewart (1954) captured and banded over 1,000 adult and juvenile clapper rails at Chincoteague; and I used it successfully in capturing clapper rails in Delaware; and king, Virginia, and sora rails at the Patuxent Wildlife Research Center, Laurel, Maryland. The trap should be placed 20 feet or so from a tidal gut, with a drift fence extending from the entrance of the trap out to the edge of the gut or across it (Fig. 42).

The all-purpose trap that I use is about 6½ feet in length. Each of the two cells is about 3×3 feet. Flattened out, each cell section is about 9 feet in length and 1½ feet in width. The rectangular top is 7×4 feet. The trap is best made of hardware cloth or welded wire. A less expensive, but less sturdy, trap can be made of 1-inch poultry mesh. The drift fence should be a minimum of 1 foot in height. One-inch poultry mesh can be used for the fence.

The gathering cage should be made of hardware cloth, and should have a ramp that begins at the opening of the cage at ground level and runs toward the top and rear of the cage. When a rail reaches the top of the ramp it drops down into a small chamber where it is well contained and easily retrieved (Fig. 43).

In the summer of 1951 at Chincoteague, R. E. Stewart (1951b) used 11 all-purpose traps between July 18 and August 31 in his clapper rail banding operation. The total number of captures was

Fig. 42. An all-purpose or cloverleaf trap with leads, placed in a marshy shrub-swamp for capturing king rails for banding. Wire mesh leads are strung out about 25 feet on each side of the trap to intercept rails as they walk through the marsh and guide them into the trap. The same trap was used for capturing clapper rails at Chincoteague, Virginia, and in the Smyrna River marshes, Delaware.

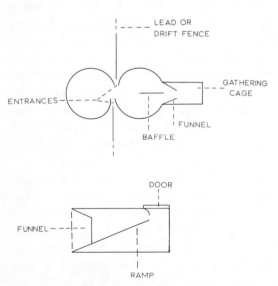

Fig. 43. Plan of all-purpose or cloverleaf trap. Side view of gathering cage (bottom). Illustration: Nancy Coon.

1,038. The largest number of captures for one trap was 248; and the largest number in one trap at one time was 17 (all nearly fully grown). The all-purpose trap is most effective when used at low tide.

In Louisiana, Bateman (1965) has had success with drop-door traps placed along paths in marshes. Drift fences along the sides of the path were used to guide the rails toward the trap. And in South Carolina, Blandin (1963) has used drop-door traps at nests to capture incubating rails. Waterfowl nest traps designed by Sowls (1949) can also be used for that purpose.

During spring or flood tides, it is sometimes possible, while working from a boat, to capture rail chicks with a crab net. In New Jersey, spotlighting at night from an airboat or outboard motorboat was used in capturing rails with a hand net at high tide (Mangold, 1974).

In his banding operations, Granville Ross of the Virginia Commission of Game and Inland Fisheries, has captured as many as 100 juvenile clapper rails in one day, using an airboat and a crab net (Forney, 1983).

Appendix 4.

METHODS OF CENSUSING
CLAPPER RAILS

Censusing clapper rails can be difficult because of the birds' secretiveness and unpredictability, their extensive habitat, and the character of the habitat. Methods employed have included call counts, nest counts, track counts, and counting the birds themselves. Some combination of these methods may be used. For example, in the Audubon Christmas Counts, calls and sightings are used. During the breeding season, nest counts from year to year will show relative abundance and trends.

I have found that in winter at Chincoteague, Virginia, when clapper rails are much less abundant, track counts may be practical. The rails tend to have fairly stable feeding territories along tidal guts, and at low tide their tracks are readily found, if the birds occur there. Farther south, in South Carolina, Georgia, Florida, and the Gulf Coast, the birds are abundant, and there would probably be too much overlapping in movements.

A practical method of censusing over an extensive area would seem to be by tallying calls. This is best done during the breeding season, when the birds are territorial and most vociferous. The best time to make such counts would be determined by spending a lot of time in the area during both day and night. There is usually some calling shortly after dawn and shortly before dusk, but such times may not always be when most of the calling occurs during a 24-hour period in a given area. In an area where I have heard constant calling at 9:00 P.M. or 10:00 P.M. by a dozen or more birds, the following morning at 8:00 A.M. I heard only 2 or 3 birds. Several factors apparently determine when calling takes place, i.e., the weather and the stage of the courtship period. Some authors have suggested that calling may be associated with the stage of the tide, particularly when the tide has turned and is beginning to go out or ebb. In my work at Chincoteague I have not found such an association to be consistent. When a clapper rail is startled in any manner, a chain reaction may occur that sometimes results in calling throughout the marsh.

During the courtship and mating season, one can depend on hearing the mating call at some time during each day and night, and at high or low tides, or in between. During the same period the primary advertising call is also frequently given. This is the call heard at all seasons and the one heard most often on Christmas Counts. Less frequently, a distress call or some other call of the clapper rail may be heard at any season. R. E. Stewart noted that clapper rails often call more on hazy or foggy days (personal communication).

The use of tape-recorded calls apparently has shown some measure of success in censusing Yuma clapper rails in Arizona by R. L. Todd, and the northern clapper rail in New Jersey (Mangold, 1974). While a tape-recorded call will usually start other birds calling, in some instances only a part of the population in an area will respond; whereas, at a later time that day in that same area, a dozen birds may be calling when a tape has not been played. In late April at Chincoteague at 9:00 P.M. I heard 17 clappers calling (a tape was not used). The next night at the same place and time with a tape-recorded call, only 6 responded to the tape.

Indicative of Mangold's success in censusing clapper rails in New Jersey, with a tape recorder and a four-foot parabolic reflector, are the results he obtained in a marsh on Drag Sedge Island. Mangold knew of the approximate number of nests in that area in 1969. Thus it was estimated that there were 10 pairs of birds. On 5 evenings, counts of calling individual birds indicated 7, 7, 9, 10, and 15 birds. In 1970, an estimated 18 pairs were present. Calling indicated 11, 17, 12, 17, and 16 birds. In 1971, an estimated 19 or 20 pairs were present. Calling indicated 18, 20, 12, and 18, on different evenings. Mangold stated that it is not known which bird of a pair calls, but it was assumed to be the male. Both male and female call at all seasons. However, the mating call is given mainly by the male, and he calls much more often than the female during the breeding season. Both sexes give the primary advertising call and various other calls.

In my experience, only by spending a lot of time in a given area during the courtship and mating season can one obtain an idea of the size of a population.

Appendix 5.

SCIENTIFIC NAMES OF ANIMALS AND PLANTS MENTIONED IN TEXT

Birds

Bittern, least *(Ixobrychus exilis)*
Blackbird, red-winged *(Agelaius phoeniceus)*
Brant, Atlantic *(Branta bernicla)*
Crow, fish *(Corvus ossifragus)*
Dowitcher, short-billed *(Limnodromus griseus)*
Duck, black *(Anas rubripes)*
Egret, great *(Casmerodius albus)*
Egret, snowy *(Egretta thula)*
Falcon, peregrine *(Falco peregrinus)*
Gadwall *(Anas strepera)*
Gallinule, purple *(Porphyrula martinica)*
Goose, greater snow *(Chen caerulescens atlantica)*
Grackle, boat-tailed *(Quiscalus major)*
Gull, great black-backed *(Larus marinus)*
Gull, herring *(Larus argentatus)*
Gull, laughing *(Larus artricilla)*
Hawk, marsh *(Circus cyaneus)*
Heron, great blue *(Ardea herodias)*
Heron, Louisiana *(Egretta tricolor)*
Ibis, glossy *(Plegadis falcinellus)*
Owl, short-eared *(Asio flammeus)*
Plover, black-bellied *(Pluvialis squatarola)*
Plover, Wilson's *(Charadrius wilsonia)*
Rail, black *(Laterallus jamaicensis)*
Rail, clapper *(Rallus longirostris)*

Rail, king *(Rallus elegans)*
Rail, Virginia *(Rallus limicola)*
Rail, yellow *(Coturnicops novaboracensis)*
Sora *(Porzana carolina)*
Sparrow, Savannah *(Passerculus sandwichensis)*
Sparrow, seaside *(Ammodramus maritimus)*
Sparrow, sharp-tailed *(Ammodramus caudacutus)*
Sparrow, song *(Melospiza melodia)*
Sparrow, swamp *(Melospiza georgiana)*
Tern, Forster's *(Sterna forsteri)*
Whimbrel *(Numenius phaeopus)*
Willet *(Catoptrophorus semipalmatus)*
Wren, marsh *(Cistothorus palustris)*
Yellowlegs, lesser *(Tringa flavipes)*

Mammals

Armadillo *(Dasypus novemcinctus)*
Deer *(Odocoileus virginianus)*
Mouse, field *(Microtus pennsylvanicus)*
Muskrat *(Ondatra zibethica)*
Nutria *(Myocastor coypus)*
Raccoon *(Procyon lotor)*
Rat, rice *(Oryzomys palustris)*
Skunk *(Mephitis* sp.)
Vole, meadow *(Microtus pennsylvanicus)*

Reptiles and Amphibians

Frogs *(Rana* sp.)
Moccasin, cottonmouth *(Agkistrodon piscivorus)*
Terrapin, Diamondback *(Malaclemys terrapin)*

Insects

Beetle, predacious diving (Dytiscidae)
Beetles (Coleoptera)
Cricket (Gryllidae)
Grasshopper (Orthoptera)
Ichneumid (Ichneumonidae)
Plant hopper (Membracidae)

Stinkbug (Pentatomidae)
Wasp (Hymenoptera)

Crustaceans

Crab, blue *(Callinectes sapidus)*
Crab, common fiddler *(Uca* sp.)
Crab, horseshoe *(Limulus polyphemous)*
Crab, red-jointed fiddler *(Uca minax)*
Crab, rock (Crustacea)
Crab, square-backed fiddler *(Sesarma reticulatum* and *S. cinereum)*
Crayfish *(Cambarus* sp.)
Shrimp, burrowing *(Crustacea)*

Mollusks

Clam, baltic *(Macoma balthica)*
Shell, fat dove *(Anachis obesa)*
Snail, periwinkle *(Littorina irrorata)*
Snail, saltmarsh *(Melampus bidentatus)*

Other

Spiders *(Arachnida)*
Worm, clam *(Nereis* sp.)

Plants

Bulrush, saltmarsh *(Scirpus robustus)*
Cordgrass, big *(Spartina cynosuroides)*
Cordgrass, saltmarsh *(Spartina alterniflora)*
Cordgrass, saltmeadow *(Spartina patens)*
Groundsel-bush *(Baccharis halimifolia)*
Hightide-bush *(Iva frutescens)*
Needle rush *(Juncus roemerianus)*
Oak, live *(Quercus virginiana)*
Rice, domestic *(Oryza sativa)*
Rice, wild *(Zizania aquatica)*
Saltgrass *(Distichlis spicata)*
Three-square, Olney *(Scirpus olneyi)*

REFERENCES

Adams, David A., and Thomas L. Quay. 1958. Ecology of the Clapper Rail in Southeastern North Carolina. *Journal of Wildlife Management* 22: 149–56.

American Ornithologists' Union. 1957. *Check-List of North American Birds.* 5th ed. Baltimore, Maryland: The Lord Baltimore Press, Inc.

———. 1983. *Check List of North American Birds.* 6th ed. Lawrence, Kansas: Allen Press, Inc.

Audubon, John James. 1835. *Ornithological Biography.* Vol. 3. Edinburg, Scotland: Adam and Charles Black.

Bateman, Hugh A., Jr. 1965. "Clapper Rail Studies on Grand Terre Island, Jefferson Parish, Louisiana." Master's thesis, Louisiana State University School of Forestry and Wildlife Management.

———. 1966. The Clapper Rail of Louisiana's Coastal Marsh. *Louisiana Conservationist* 18: 5–7, 10.

Bent, Arthur C. 1926. *Life Histories of North American Marsh Birds.* U.S. National Museum Bulletin 135. Washington, D.C.: Smithsonian Institution.

Blandin, Warren W. 1963. Renesting and Multiple Brooding Studies of Marked Clapper Rails. *Seventeenth Annual Conference of Game and Fish Commissioners.* Hot Spring, Arkansas.

———. 1965a. *Marsh Hen Investigation.* Annual Progress Report, Project W-31-R. South Carolina Wildlife Resources Department.

———. 1965b. *Clapper Rail Studies in South Carolina.* A Preliminary Report with Particular Emphasis on Productivity, P-R Project W-31-R. South Carolina Wildlife Resources Department.

Buchalew, John H. 1982. Middle Atlantic Region, ed. H.T. Armistead. *American Birds* 36:963.

Bull, John. 1964. *Birds of the New York Area.* New York: Harper and Row Publishers, Inc.

Byrd, Mitchell A., Gary Seek, and Bill Smith. 1971 Late Clapper Rail Nests. *Raven* 42:68.

Chapman, Frank M. 1940. *Handbook of Birds of Eastern North America.* New York: D. Appleton-Century Company.

Crawford, Robert L., Storrs L. Olson, and Walter K. Taylor. 1983. Winter Distribution of Subspecies of Clapper Rails *(Rallus longirostris)* in Florida with Evidence for Long-Distance and Overland Movements. *Auk* 100: 198–200.

Fargo, William G. 1927. Feeding Station Habit of Fish Crow. *Auk* 44: 466.

Farner, Donald S. 1960. Digestion and Digestive System. In *Biology and Comparative Physiology of Birds,* ed. A.J. Marshall. New York: Academic Press, Inc.

Ferrigno, Fred. 1957. Clapper Rail Study. In *Investigations of Woodcock, Snipe and Rails in 1956. Special Scientific Report—Wildlife No. 34.* Washington, D.C.: U.S. Fish and Wildlife Service.

Forney, Dennis. 1983. Hunting Clapper Rail Birds. *Heartland of Del-Mar-Va* 9, no. 2: 34–35. (Heartland Publications, Ltd., Denton, Maryland).

Greenlaw, Jon S., and Richard F. Miller. 1983. Calculating Incubation Periods of Species That Sometimes Neglect Their Last Eggs: the Case of the Sora. *Wilson Bulletin* 95: 459–61.

Grimes, Samuel A. 1944. Birds of Duval County. *Florida Naturalist* 17: 57–68.

Harris, Van T. 1952. *Muskrats on Tidal Marshes of Dorchester County.* Publication No. 91. Solomons Island, Maryland: Chesapeake Biological Laboratory.

Heard, Richard W. 1983. Observations on the Food and Food Habits of Clapper Rails *(Rallus longirostris* Boddaert) from Tidal Marshes along the East and Gulf Coast of the United States. *Gulf Research Reports* 7, no. 2: 125–35. Ocean Springs, Mississippi: Mississippi-Alabama Sea Grant Consortium and Gulf Coast Research Laboratory.

Hochbaum, H. Albert. 1944. *The Canvasback on a Prairie Marsh.* Washington, D.C.: American Wildlife Institute.

Holliman, Dan C. 1981. A Survey of the September 1979 Hurricane Damage to Alabama Clapper Rail Habitat. *Northeast Gulf Science* 5: 95–98.

Howe, Marshall. 1982. Social Organization in a Nesting Population of Eastern Willets *(Catoptrophorus semipalmatus). Auk* 99: 88–102.

Howell, Arthur H. 1932. *Florida Bird Life.* Tallahassee, Florida: Florida Department of Game and Fresh Water Fish in cooperation with the Bureau of Biological Survey, U.S. Department of Agriculture.

Hoxie, Walter. 1887. Observations on Nest Building. *Ornithologist and Oologist* 12: 181–82.

Jackson, Jerome A. 1983. Adaptive Response of Nesting Clapper Rails to Unusually High Water. *Wilson Bulletin* 95: 308–9.

Johnsgard, Paul A. 1979. *Song of the Northwind.* Lincoln, Nebraska: University of Nebraska Press.

Johnson, Robert W. 1965–66. *The Ecology of the Northern Clapper Rail, Rallus longirostris crepitans* (Gmelin) *on the Salt Marshes of Southern Nassau County, Long Island, New York.* Progress Report. Ithaca, New York: Cornell University.

———. 1973. "The Ecology of the Northern Clapper Rail, *Rallus longirostris crepitans.*" Ph.d. diss., Cornell University.

Johnston, Richard F. 1956. Predation by Short-eared Owls in a Salicornia Marsh. *Wilson Bulletin* 68: 91–102.

Jorgensen, Paul D., and Howard L. Ferguson. 1982. Clapper Rail Preys on Savannah Sparrow. *Wilson Bulletin* 94: 215.

Kozicky, Edward L., and Francis V. Schmidt. 1949. Nesting Habits of the Clapper Rail in New Jersey. *Auk* 66: 355–64.

Lowery, George. 1955. *Louisiana Birds.* Baton Rouge, Louisiana: Louisiana State University Press.

Mangold, Robert E. 1974. *Research on Shore and Upland Migratory Birds in New Jersey.* Final Report. Trenton, New Jersey: Division of Fish, Game, and Shellfisheries, Department of Environmental Protection.

———. 1977. *Management of Migratory Shore and Upland Game Birds in North America,* ed. Glen C. Sanderson, 84–92. Washington, D.C.: International Association of Fish and Wildlife Agencies.

Massey, Barbara W., Richard Zembal, and Paul D. Jorgensen. 1984. Nesting Habitat of the Light-footed Clapper Rail in Southern California. *Journal of Field Ornithology* 55: 67–80.

Mayr, Ernst, and Lester L. Short. 1970. *Species Taxa of North American Birds.* Publications of the Nuttall Ornithological Club No. 9. Cambridge, Massachusetts.

Meanley, Brooke. 1953. Nesting of the King Rail in the Arkansas Rice Fields. *Auk* 70: 261–69.

———. 1956. Food Habits of the King Rail in the Arkansas Rice Fields. *Auk* 73: 252–58.

———. 1957. Notes on the Courtship Behavior of the King Rail. *Auk* 74: 433-40.

———. 1962. Pellet Casting by King and Clapper Rails. *Auk* 79: 113.

———. 1969. *Natural History of the King Rail.* North American Fauna No. 67. Washington, D.C.: Bureau of Sport Fisheries and Wildlife, U.S. Department of the Interior.

———. 1975. *Birds and Marshes of the Chesapeake Bay Country.* Cambridge, Maryland: Tidewater Publishers.

———. 1981. *Birdlife at Chincoteague and the Virginia Barrier Islands.* Centreville, Maryland: Tidewater Publishers.

Meanley, Brooke and Anna G. Meanley. 1958. Growth and Development of the King Rail. *Auk* 75: 381–86.

Meanley, Brooke, and D. K. Wetherbee. 1962. Ecological Notes on Mixed Populations of King Rails and Clapper Rails in Delaware Bay Marshes. *Auk* 79: 453–57.

Odum, Ron. 1980. *Mercury Contamination Studies.* Final Report, 219–33. Atlanta, Georgia: Department of Natural Resources, Game and Fish Division.

Oberholser, Harry C. 1937. *A Revision of the Clapper Rails (Rallus longirostris* Bodaert). Proceedings of the U.S. National Museum, vol. 84, no. 3018, 313–54. Washington, D.C.: Smithsonian Institution.

———. 1974. *The Bird Life of Texas.* Vol. 1. Austin, Texas: University of Texas Press.

Oney, John. 1954. *Final Report Clapper Rail Survey and Investigation Study.* Federal Aid Project, Georgia W–9-R. Atlanta, Georgia: Georgia Game and Fish Commission.

Peterson, Charles H., and Nancy M. Peterson. 1979. *The Ecology of Intertidal Flats of North Carolina: A Community Profile.* Prepared for National Coastal Ecosystems Team, U.S. Fish and Wildlife Service, Slidell, Louisiana. Chapel Hill, North Carolina: Institute of Marine Sciences, University of North Carolina.

Pettingill, Olin S., Jr. 1938. Intelligent Behavior in the Clapper Rail. *Auk* 55: 411–15.

Post, Will. 1981. Breeding Bird Census—Salt Marsh (Florida). *American Birds* 35: 99, 104.

Potter, Eloise F., James F. Parnell, and Robert T. Teulings. 1980. *Birds of the Carolinas.* Chapel Hill, North Carolina: The University of North Carolina Press.

Reiger, George. 1983. *Wanderer on My Native Shore.* New York: Simon and Shuster.

Ridgeway, Robert, and Herbert Friedmann. 1941. *The Birds of North and Middle America,* Part IX. U.S. National Museum. Bulletin 50. Washington, D.C.: Smithsonian Institution.

Ripley, S. Dillon. 1977. *Rails of the World.* Boston: David R. Godine.

Roth, R. R., John D. Newsom, Ted Jonan, and L. L. McNease. 1972. The Daily and Seasonal Behavior Patterns of the Clapper Rail *(Rallus longirostris)* in the Louisiana Coastal Marshes. *Proceedings 26th Annual Conference Southeastern Association Game and Fish Commissioners,* 136–59.

Sanderson, Glen C., ed. 1977. *Management of Migratory Shore and Upland Game Birds in North America.* Washington, D.C. and Urbana–Champaign, Illinois: International Association of Fish and Wildlife Agencies in Cooperation with the U.S. Fish and Wildlife Service and Office of Publications, University of Illinois.

Schmidt, Francis V., and P. A. McLain. 1951. The Clapper Rail in New Jersey. *Proceedings 7th Annual Northeastern Fish and Wildlife Conference,* 164–72. Wilmington, Delaware.

Shaw, Samuel P., and C. Gordon Fredine. 1956. *Wetlands of the United States.* Fish and Wildlife Service, U.S. Department of the Interior Circular 39. Washington, D.C.: U.S. Government Printing Office.

Shoemaker, William, and Lee Widjeskog. 1973–77. *Clapper Rail Study.* P.R. Project W–53-R. Trenton, New Jersey: Division of Fish, Game and Wildlife.

Simmons, George F. 1914. Notes on the Louisiana Clapper Rail *(Rallus longirostris)* in Texas. *Auk* 31: 363–84.

Sowls, Lyle K. 1949. A Preliminary Report on Renesting in Waterfowl. *Transactions of the Fourteenth North American Wildlife Conference,* 260–75.

Sprunt, Alex, Jr., and E. Burnham Chamberlain. 1949. *South Carolina Birdlife.* Contribution Charleston Museum: XI. Columbia, South Carolina: University of South Carolina Press.

Sprunt, Alex, Jr., and John H. Dick. 1964. *Carolina Low Country Impressions.* New York: The Devin-Adair Company.

Steirly, Charles C. 1959. Breeding Clapper Rail in James River Cord Grass Marshes. *Raven* 30: 47–48

Stewart, Robert E. 1951a. Clapper Rail Populations of the Middle Atlantic States. *Transactions of the Sixteenth North American Wildlife Conference.* Washington, D.C.: Wildlife Management Institute.

———. 1951b. Clapper Rail Studies. In *Investigations of Woodcock, Snipe and Rails in 1951.* Special Scientific Report—Wildlife No. 14. Washington, D.C.: U.S. Fish and Wildlife Service.

———. 1954. Migratory Movements of the Northern Clapper Rail. *Bird-Banding,* 25: 1–5.

Stewart, Robert E., and Brooke Meanley. 1960. Clutch Size of the Clapper Rail. *Auk* 77: 221–22.

Stone, Witmer. 1937. *Bird Studies at Old Cape May.* 2 vol. Philadelphia: Delaware Valley Ornithological Club.

Teal, John, and Mildred Teal. 1969. *Life and Death of the Salt Marsh.* Boston: Atlantic-Little Brown and Company.

Terres, John K. 1980. *The Audubon Encyclopedia of North American Birds.* New York: Alfred Knopf.

Tomkins, Ivan R. 1937. Wayne's Clapper Rail Carries Its Young. *Wilson Bulletin* 49: 296–97.

———. 1958. *The Birdlife of the Savannah River Delta.* Occasional Publication No. 4. Georgia Ornithological Society.

Van Velzen, Aldeen, and J. Fred Kreitzer. 1975. The Toxicity of p,p'-DDT to the Clapper Rail. *Journal of Wildlife Management* 39: 305–9.

Wayne, Arthur T. 1910. *Birds of South Carolina.* Charleston, South Carolina: The Charleston Museum.

Welty, Joel C. 1975. *The Life of Birds.* 2d ed. Philadelphia: W.B. Saunders Company.

Widjeskog, Lee, and William Shoemaker. 1974. "Clapper Rail Study." P.R. Project W–53-R-3. Trenton, New Jersey: State of New Jersey, Division of Fish, Game and Wildlife.

———. 1982. "II–A Clapper Rail Nesting Survey." Project W-58-R-6. Trenton, New Jersey: State of New Jersey, Division of Fish, Game and Wildlife.

———. 1983. "II-A Clapper Rail Nesting Survey. Project W-58-R-7. Trenton, New Jersey: State of New Jersey, Division of Fish, Game and Wildlife.

Wilbur, Sanford R., and Roy E. Tomlinson. 1976. *The Literature of the Western Clapper Rails.* Special Scientific Report—Wildlife No. 194. Washington D.C.: U.S. Fish and Wildlife Service.

Willey, Guy W. 1977. Herons and Rails Victims of Severe Freeze. *Maryland Birdlife* 33: 17.

Wilson, Alexander. 1808–14. *The American Ornithology.* 9 vol. Philadelphia: Bradford and Inskeep.

INDEX

Numbers in italics refer to figures.

Gargathy Bay, Va., 33, 88
Georgia, 4, 47, 48, 73, 74, 76, 77, 79, 81, 82, 96, 99, 108
goose, greater snow, 25, *28*, 43, 96
    snow, 49
grasshopper, 18, 33, 41
Gull Marsh, Cobb Island, Va., 47
gulls, herring, 49, 94
    laughing, *23*, 48, 49, 67, 70, 94-95
    nest and eggs of, *50*

herons, 25, 51, 61, 70, 86
Hog Island, Va., 84
Hog Point, Va., 12
hunting, 77-80
hurricanes, 87, 91

ibis, 51,
    glossy, 18, 25
incubation, 15, 53-54, 58, *59*, 63
interbreeding, 11-13, *14*

Jacksonville, Fla., 83, 84
Jamestown, Va., 12, 84

Long Island, N. Y., 6, 47, 58, 73, 81
Louisiana, 4, 10, 12, 15, 29, 55, 70, 91, 101, 107

marsh hawk, 71, 93-94, *95*
"marsh hen tide," 77-78
Metomkin Island, Va., 33, 88
migrating, migration, 42-43, 72-76
Mississippi, 53
molting, 68-69
mouse, field, 25, 32, 33

Nassau County, N. Y., 47, 51, 58, 82
nesting, nests, 13-*15*, 43, 46, 47-62, 63
    populations, 48, 49
    second attempts (renesting), 47, 59-60, 61, 63
    symbolic nest-building, 45-46
New England, 10, 81, 99